The JOY of spiritual FITNESS

Other Books by Ray Simpson

Before We Say Goodbye: Preparing for a Good Death
(HarperCollins)

Celtic Blessings for Everyday
(Hodder and Stoughton, UK; Loyola Press, USA)

Celtic Daily Light
(Hodder and Stoughton)

Celtic Worship through the Year
(Hodder and Stoughton)

Exploring Celtic Spirituality: Historic Roots for our Future
(Hodder and Stoughton)

Give Yourself a Holy Island Retreat
(St. Aidan Press)

A Holy Island Prayer Book
(Canterbury Press, UK; Morehouse, USA)

Soul Friendship: Celtic Insights Into Spiritual Mentoring
(Hodder and Stoughton)

The Celtic Book of Common Prayer, four volumes
(Kevin Mayhew)

a year's training programme

The JOY of spiritual FITNESS

RAY SIMPSON

illustrated by David Colman

ZONDERVAN™

GRAND RAPIDS, MICHIGAN 49530 USA

I dedicate this book to Steph, Julie, Kim
and the staff of Quest Fitness Centre, Berwick-upon-Tweed,
UK and to all people who are willing to explore fitness of
body, mind and spirit

– Ray Simpson, Holy Island of Lindisfarne
www.aidan.org.uk

ZONDERVAN™

The Joy of Spiritual Fitness
Copyright © 2003 by Ray Simpson

Requests for information should be addressed to:

Zondervan, *Grand Rapids, Michigan 49530*

ISBN 0-310-24807-8

The author asserts the moral right to be identified as the compiler of this work.

The Scripture quotations at the end of each exercise are the author's paraphrase.

All other Scripture quotations, unless otherwise indicated, are taken from the Holy Bible: New International Version®. NIV®. Copyright © 1973, 1978, 1984 by International Bible Society. Used by permission of Zondervan. All rights reserved.

All rights reserved. No part of this publication may be reproduced, stored in a retrieval system, or transmitted in any form or by any means – electronic, mechanical, photocopy, recording, or any other – except for brief quotations in printed reviews, without the prior permission of the publisher.

Interior design by Todd Sprague

Illustrations by David Colman

Printed in the United Kingdom

03 04 05 06 07 08 09 /❖ CLY/ 10 9 8 7 6 5 4 3 2 1

CONTENTS

STRONG STUFF

LIST OF ILLUSTRATIONS

The
SPIRITUAL
HEALTH
TEST

A notice in my local fitness centre warns: 'Don't rush into exercise before you have checked out your health.' It then gives a list of indicators of one's physical condition.

It's something like that with spiritual fitness. Some people who think they are super fit might actually be in a terrible condition. Or it could be the other way round.

So before you start the training programme, try the following spiritual health test.

A. Place a number in the square (1 to 4) that corresponds with the frequency for each.

> 1 Never
>
> 2 Once in a while
>
> 3 About every week
>
> 4 Daily

Does God speak to you? ☐

Do you reflect on your day before you sleep? ☐

Do you have specific times of prayer
or meditation? ☐

B. On a continuum of '0' far left to '4' far right, where would you put
   yourself right now. Place a figure on each line.

Indifference _____ Love

Dissatisfaction/envy _____ Joy

Anxiety _____ Peace

Drivenness _____ Patience

Laziness _____ Kindness

Self-centredness _____ Goodness

Unreliability _____ Faithfulness

C. Give yourself two marks for 'yes', one mark for 'not sure' and zero
   marks for 'no'.

Does your life have meaning for you? ☐

Can you experience failure
without going to pieces? ☐

Is your image of God positive? ☐

Do you feel loved? ☐

Have you made a friend of death? ☐

Over the last month have you

forgiven someone who has hurt you? ☐

got lost in wonder, love or praise? ☐

balanced mind/body/social/spirit activities? ☐

changed anything for the better? ☐

read Scripture most days? ☐

overcome or abstained from a bad habit? ☐

made or increased a friendship? ☐

learned or studied something worthwhile? ☐

kept confidences? ☐

Has the following increased (2 marks) or decreased (zero)?

Insight ☐

Inner space ☐

Daily order or rhythm ☐

Commitment to justice ☐

Emotional healing ☐

Freedom from worry ☐

Time to laugh or celebrate ☐

TOTAL ☐

The maximum mark is 100.

If you cheat, deduct the total number of marks you have awarded yourself.

If you have 100 marks, please deduct 50 marks for lack of humility.

If you have a mark between zero and 99, you are an excellent candidate for the course.

PREAMBLE

FITNESS is FOR ALL

There is something for everyone at my fitness centre.

The beer-bellied business types perform fat-reducing exercises. An executive who has entered his first marathon is into a regime to increase stamina.

Yvonne, who now has a new boyfriend, focuses on body shaping. Agnes, concerned about her mid-life arthritic twinges, concentrates on suppleness exercises, rugby players on legs and thighs, and a skinny footballer on the upper body.

Desk-bound office workers pound the cardiovascular machines. Power lifters are into strength exercises.

A staff member helps a pensioner just out of hospital to get increasing mobility in the ankles and hips. Her colleague works with a guy who seems strong and fit but his co-ordination is poor. She tells him to forget heavy weights and concentrate on agility exercises.

Two people lie on the sun bed. A trainer explains, 'There are times, even if you are training for the Mr World competition, when the body needs rest above all else.'

A poster on the wall features 'the lithe dancer'. Another in the changing room states, 'You have only truly failed if you have never tried.'

At the desk you can buy diet sheets, performance charts, protein supplements and 'timeless beauty' – a session of massage and aromatic oils – at a price.

However, one thing is missing. These fitness programmes start from the outside and stop there.

For total fitness we need to start on the inside and work outwards. Only then can we get body-mind-soul fitness.

This book is about body-mind-soul fitness. And, like a good fitness centre, it provides something for everyone.

SPIRITUAL TRAINERS

You can do this training course on your own, just as people work out in a gym on their own. But invariably, people value the guidance of a personal fitness coach. There is an equivalent person in the world of spiritual fitness.

Paul of Tarsus likened people of faith to athletes who are being coached for a race (2 Timothy 1:4, 5).

Jesus warned people that if they carried on in the same old way, they would be fit only for the scrap heap. His aim was to get people walking, climbing mountains and being able to move in the Spirit as quickly as things are blown by the wind. Yet Jesus appointed twelve people to be spiritual guides to others as he had been to them.

Spiritual seekers who attempted in the deserts the experiment of obeying God 100 per cent of the time became known as Athletes of the Spirit. Soon they were sought out as spiritual coaches or as guides to younger people.

Those who wish to explore the role of spiritual trainers further may find helpful the author's book *Soulfriendship: Celtic Insights Into Spiritual Mentoring* (Hodder and Stoughton).

THERE is a CHAMPION in EVERYONE

This notice hangs in my fitness centre:

Member of the Month

The selected member may have lost weight, made good strength or muscle gain, overcome a particular disability, have been successful in an event, or have shown a positive attitude.

There is a champion in everyone. A champion is more than a winner. Champions give their best in defeat as well as in victory, in private as well as in public. They make the best of whatever talents they have. According to one philosopher, heroes' first victories are over themselves.

Champions liberate themselves from prejudices and patterns that cramp the spirit. They transcend adversity and shine in darkness. Champions know their own value and are prey to neither fear nor flattery. A champion is willing to put ideals before money, others before self.

Champions are natural. They keep the body and soul in balance. They have the humility to know that they are not self made and the confidence to know that there are some things only they can give.

The secret of being a champion is to work at it every day.

The exercises in this book help us to do just that. They take into account modern research into personal development and psychology, but they draw deep inspiration from ancient spiritual traditions, such as the Celtic Christian tradition.

CHOOSE *your* EXERCISE *programme*

This book's exercise programme starts with gentle, warming-up exercises and ends with the serious stuff. You may, if you wish, work through it in this order.

It may, however, be better to listen to your body and soul, and choose any exercise that feels right for that particular day. Start with any exercise that attracts you. When you have tried it out, you may either ditch it as unsuitable for you, or you may continue to practise it until it becomes second nature. When you have done either of those two things, go on to another item on the menu.

Taking into account the need for rest days and that each exercise, on average, needs to be practised for about three days, this book provides a training course for a year.

Thereafter it can be repeated year by year.

Gently
DOES IT

Warm-up exercises are necessary. If you rush into heavy exercise, you are likely to strain muscle, heart or another part of your body. It is like that with the mind and spirit as well. In fact, rest is the place to begin.

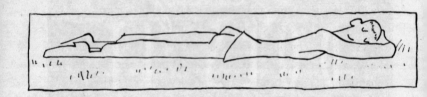

REST

Bruce Lee, the super fit martial arts expert, died young because he tried to be a top film star, business man, husband and Kung Fu master all at the same time. His physical and mental frame could not take it. The one thing he never learned was to be gentle with himself.

The beginning of spiritual fitness is to accept that no matter how hard we try, we cannot satisfy all the demands made upon us. We can learn from an example of physical training.

Angela had smoked all her adult life until two years ago. For two years she ate to compensate and became thirty pounds overweight. She went on a crash diet and exercise programme. She became exhausted and injured and was soon back where she started. Then she got a coach, who advised her to cut back and go gently. That enabled her to slowly go on improving.

It is no good doing power building if you are an exhausted wreck. Rest is what you need.

'Egyptian' P.T.

Lie down until you feel like getting up.

Breathe deeply through the stomach.

Allow yourself to sleep.

In quietness and trust shall be your strength. (1)

2
SUNBATHING

The business of living produces much wear and tear. We all have our limits. As Gary Sobers, the former hard-hitting opening batsman for the West Indies Cricket Team, once said, 'I am not a machine'.

We are not designed to go on and on giving out, without also receiving. If we try to, we end up being drained and stressed or we breakdown.

In order to live a full life, we need to be able to take in as well as to give out. And in order to take in, we need to become aware of our bodies, our feelings, the world around us and the deep things inside us.

We need to give time to it.

'Sunbathing prayer' is a way to begin, whatever climate you live in. Do not make the mistake of thinking that prayer is 'all work and no play'.

When is a good time to do the sunbathing prayer? For some people, the morning, when the sun rises, is a good time.

For others, a five minute break in the lunch hour is just what is needed. If you cannot find a quiet spot, try sitting on the loo! Or (especially if there is a queue for the loo) walk round the block until you find a place where you can do the prayer standing in a corner.

Any time will do. But the very best time is when you get that tiny nudge inside you that says, 'Watch it. You're getting fraught. Take a little break and have a sunbathe'!

Exercise

Visualize your first opportunity to sunbathe after a long, cold winter.

Wherever you are right now, find a body position that is comfortable for you. This could be sitting or lying. Breathe rhythmically.

Now in your mind and in your feelings, lie down on a beach and allow the sun to soak into your skin.

Soak in the sun. Feel it relaxing you. Feel it tingling your skin, until it moves through your whole body, warming you inside too.

Now sit in a position that is comfortable for you.

Sit cross-legged, or upright on a chair with your feet flat on the floor. Place your hands on your lap with your palms upwards, open, ready to receive.

Now focus on an image of the sun above you. But this time, the sun is the Sun of suns, the source of all energy, goodness, warmth and affection.

Feel, in your imagination, the warm rays of Love alighting upon you – filling you. Continue to breathe rhythmically.

Take time to enjoy these rays of the Sun that make you feel relaxed.

In due course, or another time, enjoy those rays that make you feel affirmed.

You can repeat and vary this exercise. You might choose rays of peace, or love, or wisdom, and so on.

My just power will rise on you like the sun and bring healing like the sun's rays. Then you will come out leaping like calves. (2)

25

3
DEEP BREATHING

What does not breathe dies. Our life is in our breath.

Our breathing should not be disconnected from our spirit

Praying in rhythm with our breathing creates good flow and helps us to pray with our whole being, not just a part of it.

If you can breathe, you can pray.

Exercise

Breathe in, breathe out.

Breathe from deep inside you, not just from the nose.

Take long breaths.

As you breathe out, let go of tensions. Feel the tension drain away. Hold the breath a little.

As you breathe in, breathe in calm.

Repeat this until you feel more relaxed.

Now wiggle your toes, then your legs, then your arms and upper body.

Become supple. Supple in body. Supple in spirit.

Exercise with words

Now use two syllable words that focus God for you in time with your breathing.

Take these three words as an example – Father, Jesus, Spirit:

> Fa (breathe in) - ther (breathe out)
>
> Je (breathe in) - sus (breathe out)
>
> Spir (breathe in) - it (breathe out)

Practise this.

You can go on to use breathing prayers that are a simple request in the same way. For example:

>Cleanse me.
>
>Calm me.
>
>Fill me.

If your heart begins to fill up, you can respond by using breathing prayers which are like words of a lover to the one they love. For example:

>Thank you.
>
>Trust you.
>
>Love you.

You can try variations, such as using just one phrase for the whole in/out breathing sequence.

Two examples

1 Breathe in and out, but make the breathing out longer.

Think of something bad that you want to drain away from you, like some rubbish that an outgoing tide takes away, and name this thing as you breathe out. Take time to become fully conscious of this. Pause after you have breathed out, and keep repeating the word until you feel that it is actually moving out of you.

Let tensions, hurts or failures flow out like an ebb tide.

Here are examples of things you might want to get out of your system, which you may name aloud or in your mind as you breathe out as follows:

>Out with envy.
>
>Out with temper.
>
>Out with gossip.
>
>Out with laziness.
>
>Out with lies.

Try this for a period. Then make your own list of the things you most want to be rid of.

2 Breathe in and out and name something good that you want to come in to you.

For example you might say:

Come in good.

Come in sweetness.

Come in peace.

Come in energy.

Come in trust.

Now make your own list and work away at it!

> There is no need to worry about tomorrow;
>
> it will have enough worries of its own. (3)

4
GOOD SELF IMAGING

Some people never enter a gym because they are ashamed or embarrassed that they are too fat, or too thin, or too clumsy, or too weak, or too young or too old.

Steph, the owner of my local gym, is a Mr Europe. He has the perfect body. Yet he gives everybody, including the old person on a zimmer frame and the young person with Down's syndrome, the feeling that they are worthwhile human beings who can improve their well-being.

Whatever our shape or size, we can start where we are, value what we have and bring the best out of it.

If you feel good about yourself, you are more likely to make progress in your quest for spiritual fitness.

Exercise

Look in a mirror.

Repeat these words: 'I see the self that God gave me to be.'

Now repeat twenty times these words, or words that come naturally to you: 'Jesus loves me this I know.'

Now say this prayer:

'I see the shadow and the light of my being.
Give me the courage to serenely carry it.'

Jesus said 'Love ... yourself'. (4)

5
POTTERING

Sometimes life is so full of other things that we have no time to get to a gym. Yet, actually, many of these other things can become our allies in keeping fit.

We can cycle to our next venue. We can climb stairs instead of using the lift. We can lift those items stored in the garage instead of lifting the bar bells. And so on.

Life can easily become one mad rush from one distraction to another. Instead of resisting them in a way that makes them worse, here is a way of handling them in a way that can become fruitful.

By turning them into prayer, they can be harnessed to creative living.

Exercise

Pottering prayer is mumbling while we're bumbling; we mumble to ourselves and to God, and we're not always sure which is which. If we are always rushing into the next thing, we will never savour the present thing or notice the little things. Here's a taster of pottering prayer:

Thank you for this post card from Auntie Emma and that filing cabinet in the office, it's so much tidier . . .

I'm glad the loo's got that new colour. I don't like the musty bit of carpet, but thank you that at least I'm nice and warm . . .

Here's the postman. Oh, dear, more bills? Now don't be miserable. Thank you, Lord, for the postman who connects us every day with people from overseas, even with the Electricity Company . . .

I'm sweaty and I smell. Thank you Lord for giving us bodies that let us know what's happening to them. I'd better have a shower. Thank you for water and for hot showers. And I mustn't forget the cotton-pickers in Asia who have made possible this nice big towel . . .

The neighbour's yard is an eyesore. But I don't have to look at it all the time. Thank you, Lord, for the honeysuckle clambering over *my* fence. That reminds me, I must get those summer plants re-potted. Thank you for pots and summer and flowers and for reminding me of things.

Now you've had a taster, start bumbling and mumbling yourself. Things you've never thought of before will come into your prayers.

> *Whoever is faithful in little things will be faithful in large ones.* (5)

6
WITH THE EBB AND FLOW

When we are at a low ebb we might

take vitamin pills

drink a lot of fluids

exercise

plan or dream of something nice

take it out on others

or give up.

We can also pray. But be warned, praying in the usual way probably won't work. Why? Because everything becomes a drain on energy.

You need a change, including a change in your pattern of prayer. So what's to be done?

Exercises

1. Accept the low ebb. Breathe deeply, offering this ebb tide to God.
2. Find somewhere or something (e.g. to read, to watch, to listen to) that nourishes you, and offer this as your prayer, feeling gratitude and believing that a restoring process is at work, all given by God.

Restore to us again the joy that comes from you. (6)

7
MELTING

$\mathcal{S}$ome people won't even limber up because they are frozen stiff.

Our personalities can be frozen too.

Something in us cries out, unspoken, 'How do I melt? It seems so impossible.'

Exercise

Think of yourself as a large block of ice.

Sure, it's too deeply frozen to melt down right now.

So focus on the edges. Watch them begin to melt.

Drip, drip, drip.

Repeat this prayer:

Thaw me out, Lord
Bring warmth to bear

During the day pay attention to what you *do* feel.

At the end of the day, ask yourself what drips have melted.

A drip can represent an emotion, a way of relating or of speaking, a sexual response.

Repeat this exercise daily until you feel, as it were, a crack in the ice.

A drip a day keeps the doctor away.

He was burning and shining (7)

TONING

Toning is about good skin texture and blood circulation and the feel-good factor.

Like an orchestra that has to tune up, spiritually fit people tone up. A good time to do this is when dressing for a new day or a new occasion.

1
WAKING

When we wake we have a choice. We can groan, 'O Lord, another day', or we can open our arms and our heart and say, 'O Lord, another day!'

It is our attitude that makes all the difference. In the uniqueness of a new day dawning, do we just get on with yet a another day, or do we truly enter into it, seeking to be aware of its fullness?

First exercise

In order to savour the difference between these two attitudes, say, 'O Lord, another day' in a 'getting on with it' way.

Now say the same words with a sense of eagerly entering a new day dawning.

Second exercise

Breathe in deeply.
Become aware of tensions.
Breathe out deeply.
Use words such as 'Thank you for the gift of sleep.'
If you were unable to sleep, say, 'Thank you for the gift of night.'
Pause.
'Thank you for the gift of a new day.'
Pause.
'All that I am I offer to you.'
Focus in turn on your head, heart, abdomen, thighs – your whole body-mind-spirit offering itself.

'All that I do I offer to you.'

Focus on as much of the day's agenda that you already know, then on what you desire to achieve this day.

'All whom I'll meet today, I offer now to you.'

In your mind bathe them, known or unknown, in love.

Try to enter each day as if you were opening the door to a room full of wonder.

> *New every morning is the love our waking and uprising prove.* (8)

2
RISING UP

Some people do rising up prayers as soon as they get out of their beds. Others do them a little later at the first suitable opportunity.

Before commencing the exercise, become aware of what you most need to let rise up within you, what you most need to reach out for. This will depend upon what has been going on in your psyche.

It is usual to say rising up prayers in triplets of phrases, taking time to meditate on each phrase.

The most famous rising up prayer is *St. Patrick's Breastplate*. Kuno Meyer's translation begins, 'I arise today through a mighty strength . . .'. The prayer refers to God, the great human qualities as lived out in Christ's life, the cosmic spiritual powers, great souls through the ages, the powers of creation and the spiritual gifts implanted within us.

These rising up prayers were common in Celtic times. It is good to make up our own. One day I made up this prayer:

I arise today
In joy of being alive
In freedom of wind
In peace of readiness

Some versions of *St. Patrick's Breastplate* use the phrase 'I bind to myself'. Echoing this, I made up this prayer on another day:

Today I bind to myself
The nurturing Parent
The befriending Christ
The blowing Spirit.

Exercise

Repeat three phrases such as the following. As you do so, make the body movements explained below.

Three phrases to use when you are in an eager mood:

'I arise today in the fullness of my (wo)manhood.'
Meditation: all that is within me stretches to be the best . . .
'I arise today in the glory of creation.'
Meditation: and I am part of that glory . . .
'I arise today in the strength of the living God.'
Meditation: God's strength is soul of my soul, flowing and rising
up in me now . . .

Three phrases to use when you are in a bad mood:
(Consciously turn your focus from being disgruntled to being positive)
'I arise today in gratitude.'
Meditation: savour things for which you are grateful . . .
'I arise today in forgiveness.'
Meditation: think of people you need to forgive . . .
'I arise today in eagerness.'
Meditation: Think of things the day may bring which you will
eagerly embrace.

Body movement for each phrase:
Raise your arms slowly above your hands, with your palms facing the sky and your fingers touching, stretching as high as you can until you feel every part of your being pulsing, reaching out for God. Hold your arms there until the meaning of the words begins to flow through your being; then slowly return your arms to your side. Repeat the action for the second and for the third phrase.

Day by day we can make up our own rising up prayers.
Now make up some of your own.

Rise up, my love, and come. (9)

3
DRESSING

Human beings put on clothes for all sorts of occasions. Every morning we get dressed. Some of us put on work or kitchen clothes.

At various times we may put on clothes for garden, cycling, fishing, jogging, surfing, swimming and other activities.

We dress up for special occasions and dress down for relaxation.

The way we put on clothes can make or mar the person who wears them.

Each time we put on or take off a garment, turn it into a prayer.

When putting on underwear, 'I put on truth in my inward parts.'

When putting on a coat before going out in to the cold, 'I put on faith to protect me from the cold winds of criticism.'

When putting on an apron in the kitchen, 'I put on the apron of humility, to serve everyone who comes here today with a smile.'

When putting on running or sports shorts, 'Help me to run straight, to go all out and to give my best.'

When getting into bed, 'Clothe me within that I may rest in peace.'

Do you get the idea? Now have a practice.

Exercise

Choose five pieces of clothing you will use this week, and weave a prayer around each.

Try to turn this into a habit (excuse the pun!).

If this way of praying works for you, keep it up day by day – or else just do it when it crosses your mind.

Write below one dressing prayer:

4
STRETCHING

$\mathcal{A}$ work-out in a gym should always begin with stretching exercises. To rush into heavy exercise without stretching, as we have said, is asking for trouble.

Exercise

Stretch both arms as high as you can above your head. Hold them there. Reach for the sky. The sky is the limit. Think about what you are to reach for today. Gradually lower your arms.

Put your feet together and stretch down to touch your toes. Instead of touching your toes, touch the ground in front of them, the ground on which you stand. Your skin is connecting with something solid, like a floor or the earth. Gradually stand erect with your arms loose at your side. Relax.

Now do this four times, facing the four corners of the earth in turn.

Face north.

Offer your ancestors to God – those you are linked to through blood and those you feel a spiritual kinship with.

Face east.

Offer your living relatives.

Face south.

Offer your past life from the womb to the present time.

Face west.

Offer the people you are with, the concerns of your heart, the things you have to do today.

You can take time over each or any of these four corners. For example, as you face south you might pray:

Bless the parts of me I've neglected.
Bless the people I've neglected.
Bless the knowledge I've neglected.
Bless the created things I've neglected.

You can vary the themes. For example, you can offer:

the world

your faith community

your family

your work

God will send messengers to earth's
four corners to gather everyone. (11)

5
FRESHENING UP

If you are drowsy through lack of air, open a window.

If you have a lack of energy that is not caused by illness, replace the nutrients, the lack of which cause lethargy. Eat food or take vitamin supplements. Also imbibe nourishment for your emotions.

If you are stale through lack of varied company, contact a friend or visit a place of interest.

If your brain is in a fixed mental circuit, get out of the circuit. Read or do something different.

It is the same with prayer and meditation. Our personalities have a strong side, which we constantly use, and a weak side, which often lies dormant and underused.

If you are stale, change the way you meditate; activate an underused part of your imagination.

Exercise

If you are stale, listen to the weak, underused side of your personality. Feed it. Exercise it.

If you are in a rut, meditate on horizons that open up.

Watch the staleness flee!

If you trust me you will rise with wings like eagles. (12)

6
COMING ALIVE

To come alive we have to reach wide, high, low and long.

Exercise

Relax. Stand feet apart, if possible with bare feet, knees slightly bent forward. Let the ground hold your feet until you feel connected to it. Breath deeply, focusing your breathing on a point about three fingers below your navel. Consciously relax the muscles in each part of your body in turn.

Reach for the skies. Bring your feet together, raise your arms above your head, with the palms of your hands horizontal and skywards. As you do so, think of your body, mind and spirit stretching to their full potential, reaching for the skies.

Lower your arms gently as you breathe out and keep on repeating this.

Stretch your arms level with your shoulders and turn back and forth, but not moving below your waist.

Think of yourself as giving out all you have.

Place your legs more widely apart until you feel the tingle of energies opening up in your inner thighs. Exult in these energies, inviting God's Spirit to animate them.

Return your feet to the first position, your legs not quite so widely apart. Arrange your arms as if you are hugging a tree. Identify yourself with God, who is hugging the world.

Feel the fullness of life and compassion flow in you and from you into the ground and back into your feet and through the air into your ears, eyes, mouth and heart.

7
WISING UP

Part of a toning process is to get wise to the ways of fitness.

But a 'know-all' in a gym is a bore and a menace. He or she takes no notice of the fitness coaches or of fitness fact sheets.

In life, wisdom lies in accepting that we are not God. The enemy of wisdom is thinking I have arrived when in fact there is a journey I have barely begun.

Exercise

Step one: Visualize a bull in a china shop. In what ways might you be just a teeny bit like that bull?

Step two: Accept that the beginning of wisdom is reverence for the other. That life is not a problem to be solved but a mystery to be entered into.

Look for this mystery in the little things.

Turn aside. Ponder.

Step three: Listen . . .

to the fragile feelings, not to the clashing fury
to the quiet sounds, not to the loud clamour

to the steady heartbeat, not to the noisy confusion
to the hidden voices, not to the obvious chatter
to the deep harmonies, not to the surface discord

Anon

Step four: Focus on what's really important.

Make a list of things you strive to acquire. Delete those that you cannot take with you when you leave this life. Add to this list (if anything is left) what you regard as 'eternal treasure'.

Now set these before you as your goals for the rest of your life.

Don't store up things that woodworm can destroy or thieves can steal.

Store up treasures that last for ever.

Your heart will be where your treasure is. (14)

DANCING

An appealing poster of a lithe dancer graces my fitness centre. Lithe legs and joie de vivre make an attractive combination.

It is said that life itself is meant to be a dance. If so, spiritual fitness requires our spirits to dance.

1
GET GOING

In order to start any journey we have to leave certain things behind, for a short or a long period – the comfortable easy chair, favourite pictures, the TV, home, garden, familiar faces. If we are physically able to, but never venture outside the house, we are classified as sick or dysfunctional.

If life is a dance, what are we doing stuck in a rut? How can we become free to make our inner journey?

In order to get out of the rut, it is good to ask, 'What are the things I must leave behind in order to be free to take the right next steps in my life?' We might need to leave behind negative attitudes towards particular people or compulsive habits.

Exercise

Say aloud: 'I leave behind . . . ' (name habits you regret).
Write down some habits you wish to leave behind:

Now hold a stone tightly in your hand. As you look at the stone, ask yourself, 'What am I holding on to in my life that I need to leave behind today?'

Walk around until you can identify this.

When you have finished, keep walking until you become willing to let it go.

Now lay the stone before a special place, such as a cross.

Think of something else you are holding on to and repeat the exercise with another stone. Repeat this exercise until you sense that you are no longer holding on to anything that is inappropriate.

Make up a prayer to accompany your actions with the stones. Here is an example.

Lead Me

from blame to blessing
from prattle to listening
from bossiness to service
from possessiveness to hospitality
from being right to just being
Now make up your own prayer:
Lead me from . . . .
Lead me to . . . .

Lead us. (15)

2
MOVE WITH MUSIC

$\mathcal{E}$xperiments with plants, animals and humans have shown that appropriate music often improves performance. Even cows produce more milk when music is played.

Exercise

Find a space where you can listen to music that inspires you.

To begin, you may do a few physical jerks and let the music be merely a background.

But before long, become attentive to the feelings the music evokes.

Now, as far as you are able, let your body express your feelings. Move with the music of your sound box and your soul.

You feel joy? Stretch wide your arms and legs.

You feel delight? Wave and jig.

You feel an overcomer? Adopt the warrior position.

You feel awe? Bow your head or kneel.

You feel thoughtful? Sit or stand.

You feel excited? Stamp your feet and clap your hands.

You feel fired up? Start marching.

You feel wonder? Place a little thing (e.g. a stone or marble or leaf) in the palm of your hand and gaze at it as you wonder.

You feel loved? Cross your hands over your heart.

You feel struck down? Lie prostrate on the ground.

You feel released? Leap, dance and shout aloud.

> Even the lame will leap and dance and those
> who cannot speak will shout for joy. (16)

53

3
CIRCLING

$\mathcal{M}$aking a circle is a human practise that reflects a rhythm of creation. Sundials remind us that the sun goes round in a circle. Ancient peoples, realizing that the sun was a source of light, warmth and blessing, walked round their crops or homes sunwise in a circle, asking the sun to bring its blessing to them. When Celtic people came to believe in one God, they carried on this idea, but prayed to the one God, whom they called the Sun of suns.

People still do this. You can physically walk round a person, thing or place that you want to pray for.

Or you can stretch out your arm and your index finger and turn it round 360 degrees.

Or you can just make a circle in your mind.

As you make a circle in one of these ways, you ask that bad things are kept out of the circle and good things are kept within it.

Here is a typical circle prayer.

Keep evil out
Keep good within.
Keep hatred out
Keep peace within.
Keep fear without
Keep hope within.

You can learn and pray this anytime, anywhere. For example, you can circle the person squashed up against you on a bus or train, or you can circle a car in a traffic jam.

You are frightened to be alone or to go out alone in the dark. You could pray:

Circle me
keep fear without
keep peace within

If someone you care about is trying to come out of drug or alcohol addiction. You could pray:

Circle them
Keep denial without
Keep honesty within.

Exercise

Think for a moment of what most concerns you today. Write or say a circle prayer that names this concern and the opposite to the problem – the quality that will help overcome it.

Circle . . .
Keep . . . . out
Keep . . . . within

Next, think for a moment what person you are most concerned about, and make a circle prayer for them.

Another time, make a circle prayer for a place, for example, your home.

Another time make a circle prayer for a situation, for example a tragedy that is on the TV screen.

If the circling way of prayer works for you, why not say a circle prayer every day?

It's really good if you continue to make circle prayers even when things are going smoothly!

As mountains surround a city, so you surround us. (17)

4
THANKING

There are two ways to respond to any situation:

Two folk behind prison bars.
One saw mud,
The other stars.

Most of us slide into the *bad* habit of taking too much for granted. We live in a complaining culture. So we need to start an alternative habit that reverses this trend.

An ancient saying is 'Gratitude is the root of all virtue'.

The German mystic Meister Eckhardt once suggested that if the only prayer we ever said was 'thank you' it would still be enough.

We cannot give thanks *for* everything, of course, since some things are bad. But we can give thanks *in* everything.

The easiest and simplest way is to do what the old children's song suggests:

Count your blessings.
Name them one by one.

If you are excited by something on the internet, video or TV, you might give thanks for the variety of human life.

If you are enjoying the thrills of a sport, you might give thanks for the marvel of the human body or of things humans have made.

If you are being swept along by the sound and fury of living, you might give thanks for the creative possibilities open to you.

If you are sad by the loss of a familiar person or thing, you might give thanks for memories that you can treasure.

Here are some examples of things we can take for granted that we can give thanks for each day:

sleep	heat
air	shelter
life	

Exercise

Write down three everyday things you can give thanks for.

1

2

3

Practise giving thanks for these things for several days. Start to do this as soon as you wake. If you forget, do it as soon as it crosses your mind. Other good times are the lunch break and before going to bed.

When you go somewhere different, or do something nice, use this as an opportunity to count new blessings.

Give thanks in all circumstances. (18)

5

TREES

Things in nature can mirror archetypes in human nature.

For example, perhaps you notice golden leaves falling from a tree in autumn. As you become fully prescient to these and the feelings they evoke in you, you become aware that there are things in your life, like the leaves, that you can let fall away, for they have done their work. Give thanks for the things you can now leave behind.

The leaves of trees rustling in the wind speak to me about how we humans are meant to be. They show up my stiffness, forced demeanour, my precious or pressurized ways. They can lead me into prayer:

Lord, I want to rustle in the wind of your Spirit
To be flexible to your will
To be a gracious presence to others.

Stay with the trees. Just being in their presence can make you become natural and truly yourself in the presence of God.

The first feeling, evoked by something in nature, is spontaneous and quick; the second feeling, evoked by reflecting on one's inner life, takes more time. You have to let the feeling evoked by the first sink in, reflect upon it and allow the archetype to come to the surface of your mind.

Stay with the feeling of thankful discovery you have just made.

Exercise

Focus on something in creation that speaks to you.
Now reflect upon the reality in you which it speaks of.
Practise this out-in rhythm.

Look at the birds . . . observe how the flowers grow. (19)

6

SING WITH CREATION

Dancing is not just about moving; it is about the joy of life.

I love this phrase from a Christian liturgy: 'let us blend our voices with the song of creation'.

To do this we have to cock our ears to catch a particular sound, of wind or wave, beast or bird; or catch the music of flower and scent which is beyond the hearing of our physical ears. Once we are attuned to this sound, we let our spirit sing with it.

Sometimes we can do this with our mouths as well as inwardly. The first time I heard seals making themselves heard, I asked David

Adam of Lindisfarne if they were giving birth. 'No,' he replied, 'they are praising God.' A nun sat still on the rocks by the Lindisfarne seals. She began quietly to sing songs in Gaelic. Two baby seals, their curiosity, but not their fear, aroused, clambered up to her. They began to sing too. When she sang, they sang. When she stopped, they stopped.

Many people find inspiration in the sea or on an island. But most of us can't live on an island. Saint Columba's prayer 'You are my island' shows us a way of creating inside ourselves an experience that we first received in the setting of nature.

> Lord, you are my island, in your bosom I nest.
> You are the calm of the sea, in that peace I rest.
> You are the deep waves of the ocean, in their depths I stay.
> You are the smooth white strand of the shore, in its swell I
>   sing
> You are the ocean of life that laps my being
> In you is my eternal joy.
>
> Saint Columba

Exercise

Listen to the sounds around you, or look at a picture.
What do you 'hear'?
Now say a prayer based upon what is evoked in you.

Let everything that has breath praise the Lord. (20)

7
BODY MOVEMENTS

There are two main types of physical exercise:

1 Aerobic exercise builds stamina.

2 Weights exercise builds strength.

Even if you are arthritic, simply taking a brisk walk can help to keep you more supple.

A spiritual equivalent to aerobic exercise, such as walking or jogging, is to do in/out prayers as you breathe.

Here is an example:

Breathe:

In: *Thank* Out: *you*

In: *Praise* Out: *you*

In: *Fit* Out: *for you*

Perhaps you see something glorious in the sky.

You say in: 'Glo' and out: 'ry'.

You accompany this prayer with a gentle body movement. Gentle body movements, when held, exercise more than you think because of the tension created in the muscles.

Exercise

Choose a two syllable word to say as you breathe in and out.

Stretch the arms out.

Say your chosen word.

Feel a tingling – the life of God flowing through you.
Hold the position. Feel the pain.
Repeat the exercise, choosing a different word.

Be like a gazelle. (21)

FOCUS

Sports people know that the difference between effective and ineffective performance often depends upon the degree to which we are focused.

We can't wallow in the past or worry about the future and also be fully focused on the task in hand.

1
THE PRESENT MOMENT

Sometimes in life we try to hang on to the past. That is useless; the past is gone.

We worry about the future. That is useless, for it will pass in a flash and then it too will be the past.

Is life then nothing? Is there nothing to live for?

There is the present moment.

To be present with all my being to this present moment is to truly live.

Moses was reared to believe in gods who were limited to a particular time, place and people. How could he talk about the true God to the emperor of a country whose gods were different?

He had an enlightenment which solved this riddle. As Moses stood before a bush that endlessly burned in a desert a voice informed him: 'Tell the Emperor that "I am-I was-I will be" has sent you.' Moses learned that God is the eternal Now.

When I become fully present, I reflect the eternal Now.

In order to reach this experience we have to practise recollection.

The result is that we are less likely to rush into the pursuit of trifles, chasing anything that catches our fancy. We are more likely to practise being fully present at each stage of the day.

Perhaps we are at a meeting. Be fully present to the person who chairs the meeting and to its purpose.

Perhaps someone keeps on chattering to us? Is the chatter mindless or does it disguise a need to be taken seriously? If so, we become aware of that person's unique history, future and present.

Perhaps we are bored by a routine job? Become fully present to the wonder of work.

Exercise

Breathe deeply and relax.

Become fully attentive to your body. What is it feeling?

Now become fully attentive to the feelings that are inside you, that are pushed down.

Now become fully attentive to what goes on around you.

Now become fully attentive to what is required of you in the period that lies ahead.

> *Love God and others with all your heart, mind, soul and body. (22)*

2
MINDFULNESS

The world seems out of joint.

Our best response is to be fully mindful in every thing we do, to direct every element of our lives to the Source and Sustainer of all.

Someone may object. 'Our type of people are suited to do several things at once; we like to keep several balls in the air at the same time . . .'

It is true that there is a co-ordinating function built into our unconscious. It is also true that there are many transitions to be made in life, and that to make good transitions we need to be aware of what we transfer to as well as what we transfer from.

Nevertheless, at the conscious level it is best and it is possible to make our primary focus one thing at a time.

Throughout today, sense what is the primary thing or person you are to focus on in each moment, and focus with all your heart.

For example, when

I eat	I work
I talk	I listen
I travel	I buy
I walk	I watch
I read	I move
I sleep.	

Say this prayer:

I am giving you love with my whole heart
I am giving you honour with my whole desire
I am giving you devotion with all my senses
I am giving you being with my whole mind
I am giving you my best thoughts, my deeds, my words,
my will, my understanding, my intellect, my journey, my end.
Carmina Gadelica (adapted)

Whatever you do, do it from the heart, to God. (23)

3
MAKING EACH THING COUNT

Kenneth Ring, in his book on near death experiences, came to realize that 'every single thing that you do in your life is recorded and that even though you pass it by not thinking at the time, it always comes up later.'

This kind of experience echoes insights recorded in Scripture. The Book of Revelation pictures a Book of Life in which all our deeds are recorded.

People who have a near death experience speak of a review of their life that takes place in the presence of a being of light. This review reveals that the only truly valuable goals in life are learning to love others and to grow in wisdom.

Exercise

Keep before you throughout this day a mental picture of each thing you do being recorded in the presence of a being of light and love.

Each time you do something ask yourself: Is it appropriate? Is it necessary? Do I do this with thought? With attention to detail? With love?

Include the smallest things, such as what you do with a sachet of sugar or salt.

4
PULLING THINGS TOGETHER

My mind is full of ideas. My body is full of energies.
So many choices lie before me. Possibilities seem endless.
Other people put so many expectations upon me.
Days are too short. I am pulled in all directions.
Life is all activity: Where is the being?
Stillness has fled: Where is the rhythm?
My life does not hang together: Where is the meaning?
I need a unifying focus: Where is God in all this?

I arrived at my local fitness centre feeling pulled in all directions. Should I give training a miss, skip through a few perfunctory exercises, or what?

A mate had come from his night shift – not the best time to be focused. He went straight for it, however. He knew what he had to do.

In your mind walk away from the immediate pressures.

Physically, or in your mind, walk to a place with a view.

Lift up your eyes to a hill, a cloud or a horizon.

Look at your life in the perspective of eternity.

In that light, what are the things you do that are not really important? Make a list of these.

Now, in your mind, let these go.

Decide that in future you will say no to invitations that lure you into the merry-go-round that has no eternal meaning.

Become aware of the deepest thing in your heart, of the most important things you have to do.

> *I will lift my eyes to the hills.*
>
> *Where will my help come from?* (25)

5

CENTRING

Winston Churchill was once brought a pudding. 'This has no theme,' he told the waiter. 'Take it away.' Our prayers can be like that pudding. Polonius' words in Shakespeare's play *Hamlet* remind us of this fact: 'My words fly up, my thoughts remain below; words without thoughts never to heaven go.' It is all too easy, even when we pray, for our thoughts to bustle in and out and then wander off.

We seem to need a mental equivalent to a magnet that gathers together scattered iron filings. Or an equivalent to the float used in fishing. Without a float to focus our attention, we would drift off and miss the moment when the fish takes the bait.

An equivalent to this in prayer is a key word that people repeat over and over again until it is repeated unconsciously. This key word has a centring effect. It gathers together thoughts that scurry in and out of the mind, and it brings the wandering mind back to the theme.

Some people use a name of God as their focus word that they repeat over and over again. Or they may use an ancient Aramaic word such as *Alleluia* which unites in praise people of all languages. A word that resonates deep in the belly as well as in the mind, and which has great centring power and meaning is *shalom*.

This Hebrew word is sometimes translated as 'peace', but it means much more than that. It means the deep harmony of the total person with God, the human community and the environment.

Exercise

As you breathe out say 'shalom'. The last part of the word should be drawn out – 'o-o-o-o-m-m-m-m' – and should accompany the long, drawn out breath. Your breathing should be from your belly. Your whole body should begin to relax; your whole being should begin to reverberate with the sound and the significance of shalom.

I will give you shalom and you will sleep without fear of anyone. (26)

71

6

BECOMING REAL

Some people in fitness centres hide their bodies under weird clothes, cover their skin in sham sun tan, shape or colour their hair in order to distract attention.

Certain body builders who artificially bloat their bodies with steroids seem to have turned their love inwards, to their own bodies. They do not find their manhood in reaching out to others. This may be because they are insecure within themselves.

They have identity problems.

In contrast to this a natural body builder told me, 'A man's got to do what a man's got to do.' He knew how to be real.

How can we get real?

Exercise

Resolve this day

> to do what is in your heart regardless of what others think;
>
> not to speak unless you have something to say – overcome that fear of silence; and
>
> to be honest about what you feel.

Check yourself against these three resolves every hour. At the end of the day give yourself a mark out of a hundred. Do not expect to achieve 100 per cent. If you achieve 10 per cent, repeat the exercise each day until you reach a standard you are happy with.

7
MAKING YOURSELF AT HOME

Most people are trying to be what they are not. They live by subterfuge.

Sometimes I am trying to be the person who will be liked by other people.

Sometimes I am trying to run away from what is inside me. I keep the lid on it, because it harbours too much hurt for me to cope with.

Sometimes I am trying to control people, because I fear that if I don't, they will control me.

Sometimes I am driving myself like a workaholic because I feel that I only matter if I am successful in the eyes of others.

Birds are not like that. Nor are trees. Nor are the serene and wise people of the great traditions.

They are at home with themselves. They are at home wherever they are, whomever they are with.

How can I be like that?

Exercise

Let your thoughts wander back to one of the first times you felt you could not be yourself. Perhaps you were tense, or angry, or shy, or ashamed, or afraid, or confused or you felt worthless.

> What did you do?
>
> Where did you place yourself?
>
> What was your body language?
>
> What were your feelings?
>
> What, if anything, did you say?
>
> How did you compensate for this bad experience afterwards?

When you have taken plenty of time to replay this scene, say 'cut', and replay the scene a second time.

Now replay this scene in your mind, but this time, let the adult inside you take the lead. Decide that this time you will make yourself at home, that you will be yourself.

In your visualization go through the six questions above. How were they different this time?

Now that you have the idea, practise being yourself throughout this day, at home, work and play.

As the sparrow builds a nest,
so I make myself at home in God. (28)

FAT BURNING

Modern societies breed overweight people. To burn off excess fat we need both the right exercise and the right diet.

Spiritual fat consists of the things that weigh down or clutter our spirit such as greed, envy, pride and temper.

Believers who went into the deserts to burn off such things became known as 'athletes of the Spirit'. They engaged in an all-out training programme against these negative, destructive passions.

The exercises that follow help us to burn off excess fat.

1
GREED

A grasping attitude is a killer.

Grasping and greed are the source of many of our problems. Giving is part of the cure.

Exercise

Take a coin in your hand. Grasp it tightly. Now let it fall from your hand.

Think of things you grasp. Repeat the coin exercise in your imagination, but substitute for it each thing that you grasp. Let each thing fall.

Repeat this exercise until you have let go of the main things you grasp at.

Now place the coin in your hand, but with your palm open and facing upwards.

It stays there without you having to grasp it.

You are offering or giving it.

Repeat this palm upward exercise in your imagination, but substitute for the coin the thing you are offering.

You are becoming a giving person instead of a grasping person.

Happiness lies in giving more than in receiving (29)

2
ENVY

When we are jealous of someone we harm not only them but ourselves. The first of the following exercises deals with the *symptom*, our attitude towards the other person.

The second exercise deals with the *cause* of jealousy, our attitude towards ourselves. When I realized that my jealousy was caused by potential in myself having been repressed, I prayed a prayer on these lines:

Lord, if I was living in my full potential,
I would have deep down satisfaction
and I'd enjoy others living in their full potential.
So I take this feeling of jealousy
as a divine cue.
You're telling me that
I'm not living in my potential.

First Exercise

Look in the eyes of the person you envy. You may do this either physically or in your imagination. As you look in their eyes, say some such thing as this: 'Bless her, make her shine . . .' or 'encourage him, make him grow'.

Repeat the prayer every time the green twinge returns.

Second exercise

Imagine God (and angels, and saints, and so on) looking down on you. What strengths and hidden possibilities do they see in you that they want to encourage?

Name these one by one and savour them.

Now say, 'I bless these in the name of the Creator, the Restorer, and Energizer.'

Pray:

Lord,
Put confidence into my being,
Put thoughts into my mind
As to what I should do now to develop
these potential strengths.

Watch out for the results!

I have come that you may have life in all its fullness. (30)

3
RAGE

A common mistake is to think that we can only pray about nice things.

Just as there are always two sides to a coin, so there is always a dark side to even the nicest person. This dark side often takes the form of anger. In some of us, this anger comes out into the open in swearing, perhaps, or in violence; in others this is repressed. If it is repressed too much, it can lead to depression or to negative behaviour.

Sometimes, we do not admit even to ourselves how much anger there is inside us. Our dreams can give us a clue: Bad dreams may indicate bad but repressed emotions.

It is best to let this anger out into the light of day. Light, that is exposure, has a healing effect. Naming out loud the objects of your anger may help to release them.

In my fitness centre there is a punch bag. If I am angry, I take it out on the punch bag before I do some 'nicer' exercise.

Some go to a counsellor to sort out their anger, but a counsellor cannot always be present just when we need one.

The best way to deal with anger is to let it out. Here is a way to do this.

Exercise

Take a stone or a piece of wood small enough to hold in the palm of one hand. Some people use a piece of wood shaped like a cross.*

Now try to crush this with all your might. Vent your anger upon this stone or piece of wood.

Hopefully, you can then begin to tell your stone, or wood, or the cross what it is that makes you so angry.

---

*Holding Crosses are available from Saint Michael's Cottage Crafts, Bowthorpe Hall Road, Bowthorpe, Norwich NR5 9AA; telephone: 01603 746106.

How you have been mistreated.

What this has done to your spirit.

How you feel about those who have made you angry.

What is happening to your body and to your spirit.

The best way is to speak out your anger to some one you can trust. As we build up our capacity to trust, we diminish the hold of anger over us.

That is why the use of a holding cross has such great value. You are crushing and speaking out to the Person the cross represents.

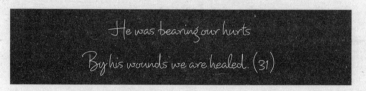

He was bearing our hurts

By his wounds we are healed. (31)

4
ATTENTION-
SEEKING

I have a craving to be noticed. It is getting to me.

I hear myself thinking, *Why was I not invited?* or *Why didn't they speak to me?*

All day long and at night I feel left out. I am becoming touchy.

Everyone else is into assertiveness and marketing and socializing. They often do these things in the most sophisticated ways.

Why should I be treated as a nobody?

My thoughts move from self pity into working out how I can make my mark. How I can get their attention.

My inner energy becomes hostage to this pathetic motive.

But what can I do about it?

Curbing the worst symptoms will lead nowhere.

Better to go the root of the problem. I need to rediscover a sense of well being deep within me. Like a baby contentedly feeding at its mother's breast.

Then I can be myself.

Exercise

Throughout this day and night, repeat the saying below.

I will repeat these words as I nestle in the arms of God, my Source.

I will repeat these words in my head as I walk tall.

I will repeat these words in rooms full of babble and as folk greet one another, and I shall feel good.

> *I am like an infant nestling in its mother's arms.* (32)

5
PRIDE

Humanity has been described as a collection of colliding egos. For much of my life I liked to think that I was the exception. Now I know better.

The ego has been described as the driving seat of the selfish part of a human being.

Most people don't know that they are run by their ego.

The fact that you do know means you are now at the starting post. The exercise can begin.

It is a game called Hunt the Ego.

Exercise

Recall that in past centuries various empires published maps of the world with their own country in the centre. For example, China produced maps in which China was in the centre and every other country was labelled 'barbarian' and lumped together under a different colour.

We do much the same as individuals. We assume our ego is the centre of the world and we arrange everything else around it.

Imagine that everything you think, feel and do today has to be located on a map. But instead of your ego being the centre of the map, God (as the greater good) is in the centre, which means that each thing and person now has the place on the map that is right for them.

The game is to catch each thought, word or action and decide if you are fitting these around your ego, or whether you are fitting your ego into a God centred-map of the world.

Start now, and play this game whenever your thoughts return to your ego. Ask, 'What am I thinking ? Am I trying to fit other people, my timetable, everything, around what I want . . . ?'

Practise this throughout the day, and any day when you become aware that you are in ego overdrive.

Put other's interests before your own. (33)

6
PIGHEADEDNESS

Being pigheaded is a particular form of egocentricity.

My sister once said to me, 'Why don't you accept that you behave like a pig?'

Once we accept that we can be pigheaded, perhaps the best way to deal with it is to make fun of ourselves. Learn not to take ourselves too seriously.

Exercise

Repeat this prayer or make up your own:

The first thing, Lord, is to accept that I am pigheaded.
It was stupid of me ever to think I wasn't.
I admit that there are people around me
who are less pigheaded than I am.
It's just as well to get that out of the way.
But it's not the last word for you.
You start where people are, Lord,
which means pigheaded people like me
can communicate with you.
That's a relief.
Now I've got that off my chest, what should I pray next, Lord?
Yes, of course. I will pray for each person here
(or whom I'll meet today or who are on my mind).
I will ask that they may be the person
you want them to be.
I'll build them up in my prayer.
That's good for my ego too.

I'm still a pig. But I've become a praying pig.
And a praying pig becomes a bit less selfish.
That's enough for now, Lord,
for you come in the little things.

Encourage one another. (34)

7
PREVENTION IS BETTER THAN CURE

It is one thing to burn off excess fat, but prevention is better than cure. It is better to cure the thing in us that makes us over indulge. If we don't, old habits will re-assert themselves. Unless we suffer from a purely biological malfunction, excess fat is produced by addictive eating habits. These are often a false compensation for some deeper nurture we are failing to receive.

Food is only one of many addictive cravings. Others are for

money	sex	food
power	alcohol	fame
drugs	tobacco	immortality

Each person's cravings take a distinctive form and have their own little twists.

Exercise

Answer this question: What are my deepest cravings?

Recognize that these are a misdirected form of an underlying, legitimate need. For example, underlying many of our cravings are needs for love, belonging or affirmation.

Decide which underlying need your craving is a symptom of.

Tell yourself that this is a natural, legitimate underlying need.

Having recognized you have an unmet need, invite God to fill the unmet underlying need.

In my craving for . . .

Come with your infinite love (or . . .)

> You alone are our hearts' desire. (35)

Stress
BUSTERS

We live in a stressful society. Stress is now endemic in many professions and work places. Some stress can be creative. The spiritually fit person eliminates negative stress factors and harnesses positive ones.

1
SLEEPLESS

Sleep is a precious gift. When it eludes you, don't get annoyed, for that only makes things worse. Take it as an opportunity to sort something out, to do or read something, or to pray.

Exercise

If the cause of your sleeplessness is physical, it is good to use the time to pray for others' needs. If it is caused by your distress at some situation, it is good to pray for the needs of those whose plight distresses you.

But if your inability to sleep is caused by some unresolved emotional conflict in yourself, it is more important to have an inner conversation about it. For example,

> What's behind this, God?
>
> Why am I tense?
>
> Please show me what I am bottling up that I need to let out . . .

Write down in a notebook the thoughts that come.
Then offer the things that have come to light to God.
And let sleep come.

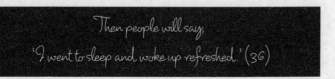

Then people will say,
'I went to sleep and woke up refreshed.' (36)

2
TRAPPED

All of us feel trapped at times.

We can feel trapped in a place, a house, a job, a relationship, a financial or cultural framework. We can even feel trapped in our own bodies.

Extroverts want to hit out when they are trapped; introverts tend to shrink into themselves. These natural reactions make matters worse. Yet prayer, which can make matters better, is not something we naturally want to do.

So it is worth getting into a daily training that deals with life's little traps. In this way we form a habit that will do well for us when we fall into a big trap.

Exercise

Make a mental picture of yourself as the smallest person in a trapped situation. Now picture yourself growing in stature, in body, emotions, and spirit. See yourself walk through the place with poise, oozing peace.

Now, or tomorrow, imagine the worst that can be done to you. Perhaps it involves loss of something dear to you, even of life perhaps. Now visualize qualities coming in to your soul such as dignity, love, peace, forgiveness, self-respect.

Remember that you can have a free spirit in any situation, however restricting it may be.

Whenever you feel trapped, place before God the process you have to go through. Pray for yourself to become magnanimous. As you pray, you gain a big spirit.

Watch for results.

3
SCREWED UP

Nine out of ten people get screwed up by someone or another. Some of us get screwed up with epidemic frequency. The reason may be that a parent or peer figure screwed us up when we were young. Perhaps they still do. If our reactions to them have never been dealt with, all sorts of innocent people may trigger them off.

Exercise - the three gardens

Visualize three gardens.

1 Place the person who most screws you up (we will call this person 'Dad') in the first garden.

Leave him there, acting out all the negative things that screw you up. Now calmly walk out of the garden, close the gate behind you, and do not look back.

2 Now put a different aspect of your 'Dad' in the second garden, your 'Dad' in the mode of someone for whom you can give thanks. Repeat prayers such as

> 'I give thanks for . . . . ' (*a memory*) or
> 'I give thanks for . . . .' (*a trait*).

Start to think of everything you can give thanks for, and spend as much time as you can speaking out these thanksgivings.

3 Thirdly, put your 'Dad's' inner child in the third garden.

Think of all the emotional resources he lacked, the emotional support in his early life he may have been denied, the handicaps he suffered from. Now pray for that child-in-your Dad. Bless him. Forgive him. Affirm him. Encourage him. Use your own words, or let such feelings flow without words.

4
VICTIMIZED

You know that however hard you try, 'they' will pick on you.

First it was one thing, then another. You sincerely tried to put those things right. After that it was something else. Then they expected you to be in one place and somewhere else at the same time.

Innuendoes started coming. 'If you don't improve . . .'

They are always judging, always trying to control.

They always assume they are spotless, and that you must get things right 100 per cent of the time.

It feels like they are ticking you off against a long check list that they make up themselves. If you get 100 per cent they'll start a different list until they can catch you out.

They try to pick a quarrel. They want you to lose your cool, to say something unbalanced, so they can get you that way. They drop hints to other people and sow seeds of dissension.

Exercise

Remember the Rule of Saint Columba: 'Constant prayers for those who trouble you.' Pray for the other person whenever the thought of them troubles you.

Never, ever, descend into a slugging match, or give 'an eye for an eye'. Stick to actual facts. Put right what you can. Apologize for mistakes.

Try to understand what lies behind their hostility towards you. Are they hurting? Or frightened? Or jealous?

Find a way to include them in your vision.

Be determined, not to become an enemy. Treat them as if they were allies.

Breathe deeply and relax into eternal love. Get your wellbeing from a source other than this person.

> Happy are those who are persecuted
> for doing what is right. (39)

5
DISTRAUGHT

A pastor called on a young couple whose only baby had just suffered a cot death. 'How can you believe in a God who can do this to us?' the mother screamed at him. He was saved from having to attempt a reply, for her partner quietly said, 'Perhaps God's hurting even more than we are.'

There are times when we desperately need to pour out our sorrows, but we feel there is no one who can understand us from the inside, so we put the lid on. This causes us damage; it can make us ill.

It is possible, once we get a right picture of God in our minds, to pour out our sorrows to God.

Jesus wept and said to people whom he knew would soon lose their babies and their homes: 'I've wanted to draw you to me like a mother hen gathering her chick' (Luke 13:34).

If the Divine Being can shed the tears of a broken heart on our behalf, we can pour out our souls to the One who understands.

Exercise

Reflect on this ancient Celtic saying: 'There is a mother's heart in the heart of God.'

Pour out your soul to the 'mother's heart in the heart of God.'

Tears are my food day and night

I pour out my soul

Yet I will hope still in my Saviour

and my God. (40)

6
EXCLUDED

When we feel excluded by other people we are tempted

to blame them   to nurse self pity

to rehearse grievances

How can we turn these reactions round?

Exercise

First, let your feeling of exclusion create empathy with millions of people who are excluded in worse ways than you are.

Empathize with those who are excluded from any of the following:

a home   a job

a decent diet   listening peers

fair pay

Second, say thank you that God is here for you, that you are being welcomed into God's loving heart and purpose.

You can do this in any way that comes naturally.

You can keep repeating the words 'thank you'.

Others praise God in song or in what Christians call 'tongues'.

Third, thank God for this opportunity of being made one with the divine but human Christ in his rejection on the Cross.

Today you will be with me in paradise

(said Jesus to a criminal about to die). (41)

7
IN BREAKDOWN

When we are near to, or in, a time of breakdown, it makes matters worse to try and think what we should do or pray about it.

In this situation we need a rope to hang on to.

Here is a way of using a rope – a prayer rope.

A prayer rope is any rope which has lots of knots in it. You can buy one or make one.

Exercise

Hold the rope in your hands. As you hang on to it, hang on also to some 'gut' prayer and keep repeating it.

One of the shortest prayers in the English language is the word 'Help!'

Or your gut prayer could be the word 'Jesus'.

Or it could be the first words of the Lord's Prayer: 'Our Father'.

Hold the first knot of the rope in your hands and repeat one of these prayers slowly, with feeling, ten times. Then go on to the next knot and repeat as before. And so on.

Hang on in there.

Underneath are the Everlasting Arms. (42)

BALANCE

I thought I was doing quite well in a range of exercises, until I asked a sports centre staff member to show me how to hold a bar behind my head. After several attempts to teach me the correct way, she said, 'You'll have to work on co-ordination.'

A person may have great energy or strength, but if they lack balance – whether on a bicycle, with a barbell or in life – they are severely handicapped.

If we want all-round spiritual fitness, and good balance, we need to develop our co-ordination. The exercises in this section help us to do this.

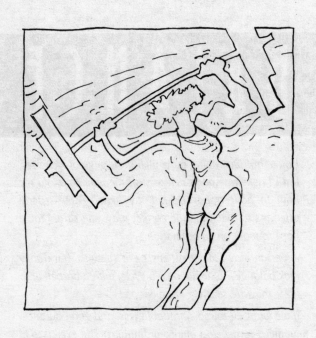

1
ON A HIGH

When we are on high, or are swept along by hype, we are in danger of losing touch with our real selves and the real world around us.

It is a good practice to pray at our big and little pinnacles of success, otherwise they may go to our heads and we may go hyper. 'Go to God for your whole diet,' said John Wesley, 'not just for medicine.' People who don't do this often head for a fall.

My fitness centre coach won an international Mr Universe competition. But he did not let it go to his head. On his return he did two things. He displayed his silver cup in the centre so everyone could share in the enjoyment. Then he cleaned the gents' toilets.

These actions illustrate two secrets of successful living:

Share our joy of achievement with others.

Then do something routine and down to earth.

Exercise

Imagine you have just climbed a pinnacle.

You get out a flag and wave it in delight.

Who are you waving it to? Visualize yourself including others and God in your celebration.

Whenever you are on a high, give a wave to God, or even a wink.

It is your way of showing you recognize that God is in the situation and in you.

What you achieve is not by your human power but by my Spirit. (43)

ON A LOW²

Often, when we are depressed, we accuse ourselves of being useless or worthless. That is the negative response. A positive response is to be gentle with ourselves, to eat vitamins that give sparkle and iron, and to wait for the return of good feeling.

While you are waiting, tell yourself: 'It's okay; I'm changing gear. It will show later.'

Exercise

Give yourself a good talking to. Tell yourself something on the following lines: 'Please remember that I am not always depressed. It is not the end of the world. It is a phase. There are probably things I can do about it.'

If you are on a low because you been overheating one side and neglecting another side of yourself, do something different.

Sleep, watch a film, read, sun bathe, exercise, have a night out, call on friends, explore something or go somewhere.

Decide what compensatory thing you need to do.

Do it.

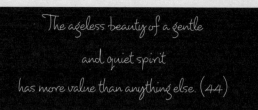

The ageless beauty of a gentle
and quiet spirit
has more value than anything else. (44)

3
SHRIVELLED

Some of us carry bits of ourselves that have long been shrivelled. We only face this fact if some trigger brings it to the surface.

Take one example. Potentially the most disastrous thing that can happen to a child is the loss of a parent – through death, emotional absence or abuse. At the stage when trust should grow that enables the child to become confident in their identity, sexuality and ability to make relationships, there is confusion and shrinking.

This inner shrinking remains throughout life unless at some stage it is acknowledged and repaired.

Neglect and abuse takes many forms, and when we encounter them, something in us shrivels.

Exercise

Make a list of four things that most make you shrivel inside:

1

2

Now visualize yourself as a shrinking person. Perhaps you can focus on an actual episode or feeling of childhood.

Repeat these words:

I bring to you the child that craves affection.
I bring to you the child that fears to trust.
I bring to you the child that shrinks at conflict.
I arise today in the power of the great Father
who brings manhood and womanhood into being.
I arise today in the power of the great Son
who surmounts the things that shrink our being.
I arise today in the power of the great Spirit who enables my
humanness to grow.

Now visualize yourself as you would be, feel and act if you'd had that trustful, non-abusive relationship earlier in life.

Act out this new image of yourself in words and deeds.

May your love and self-understanding
go on growing more and more. (45)

4
HURT

$\mathcal{E}$veryone gets hurt. We can be hurt by those who wish us well, as well as by those who wish us ill.

There are three ways of dealing with hurt.

The first way is to become hard and to hit back. This solves nothing.

The second way is to repress and hide from hurt. This stores up trouble, because the hurt festers under the surface.

The third way is to accept that we are hurting, not to cover it over, but to share our hurting self with another person or with God.

Exercise

Repeat this prayer and meditate upon it.

'Birther, affirm me as I carry this hurt.'

Take time to feel God's affirming presence strengthening every part of your being.

'Restorer, help me as I handle this hurt.'

Take time to grasp how Christ in you wishes to transcend the hurt in the way you think, feel, and speak.

'Spirit, heal me as I mend this hurt.'

Take time to sense how the Spirit moves you to reach out to the person who has caused the hurt, either physically or inwardly, so that the breach is restored as far as it depends upon you.

I will bring healing like the sun's rays. (46)

DISAPPOINTED

We have all suffered disappointment at certain times. Perhaps we have messed something up or failed a test. Perhaps it goes deeper. We perceive that others are disappointed in us, or we are disappointed in ourselves.

If we do not address this, it can blight the rest of our lives. A spirit of disappointment can prevent us from making a fresh start and reaching out to new challenges.

When disappointment rules, the best thing we can do is to face it, share it and move on from it.

Exercise

Say this prayer slowly and from the heart:

Lord, I won't pretend.
I accept the hurt of this disappointment
and I hold it before you . . .
Lord, I won't exaggerate.
It is not the end of everything.
You still love me and believe in me.
There are many other things in my life
which have not been disappointments.
I spend time now thanking you for these . . .
Lord, I won't withdraw,
though I will take time to be content
with the little things of life . . .
Lord, with you

I will look this day in the face,
I will look my fellows in the face,
I will look myself in the face.
And you will look at me.
And you are pleased.

You are my friends
I chose you to bear fruit that will last. (47)

6

PARANOID

When we are paranoid we feel as if everything conspires against us; that everyone is out to criticize, undermine, take over or attack us.

Part of this condition is that we don't easily admit to it.

So give yourself the benefit of the doubt. Whether your paranoid tendencies are slight or acute, practise combating it with the following exercise.

Exercise

At the first signs, or even before any signs of paranoia, repeat twenty times, 'I admit I might be ill'.

Part of the cure is to keep connecting with the matter-of-fact world. Slowly repeat the following words several times:

The sun is not against me.
It shines on good and bad alike.
The birds are not against me.
They sing, fly and hunt regardless of my circumstances.
Not everyone out there is against me.
I will meet people in shops, streets or on screens who reflect
your image and who will wish me well.
You are not against me, dear God.
Your love, your self giving
excludes no one, and enfolds even me

If feelings of persecution torment your soul repeat these words over and over again, 'I am enfolded in your love'.

Your love is so great that we are called your children. (48)

7
SUICIDAL

*I*t's surprising how many of us entertain suicidal thoughts when we have our backs to the wall. For most us, these thoughts are a coping mechanism, and we know we will not actually carry them out.

One of the best treatments for suicidal tendencies is humour.

A mother told a Church Army Captain that she was about to commit suicide. The Captain, preoccupied with other things, was not paying attention. 'Oh good,' he said absent-mindedly. The mother thought this was so funny she could not stop laughing. The idea of suicide went out of her mind.

If you feel suicidal, remember, before you do anything silly, some good things you still have, however awful your situation may be.

Here is a list I made when I was feeling suicidal:

the gift of life today	sunshine
vision	experience
achievements	the possibility of growing as a person
God	memories of loving relationships

Also remember that you have not truly failed if you start to build with the rubble that is left after a disaster.

Exercise

Make a list of good things in your life.

Imagine how your life is like a waste ground. What is the rubble in your life? With what can you start to build?

Build one thing today, even if it's a friendly sentence. Repeat this tomorrow, and so on.

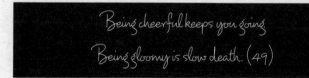

Being cheerful keeps you going.
Being gloomy is slow death. (49)

Stamina
BUILDING

A physical fitness programme can be threatened by many factors: illness, accident, new duties, over-busyness, the lure of alternative lifestyles, criticism, boredom and loss of motivation.

Progress in our spiritual fitness can also be undone. Our spirits can be dragged down by exhaustion and distractions.

We need to see these as hurdles to be overcome. We need to see ourselves as potential champions training to defeat every onslaught. Each of us can have a 'gold medal' that will long outlast this life.

Sometimes we just need to keep on keeping on. At other times we need to change our routines. Either way, we need to develop stamina.

The following exercises will help us to do this regular Bible study above all.

1
NO GAIN
WITHOUT PAIN

*L*ife is hard; it is not a bed of roses. Once we accept this, however, life ceases to be a problem and becomes a path. The key to a life of fulfilment is to face problems head-on, however painful.

A prominent poster in my fitness centre reminds everyone 'No gain without pain'.

Suffering is built into the universe. It is essential to our evolution as human beings.

Most of us get into a bad habit. We do the easy thing that gives us pleasure now and put off necessary but painful action until another day. In this way we become flabby.

The cure is to replace the principle of instant gratification with the principle of delayed gratification. This requires us to schedule things so that we experience the pain first and the pleasure that follows then lasts longer.

This lesson can be learned quite early in life. By the age of twelve, some children are able without any parental prompting to complete their homework before they surf the net.

It is not too late to learn now.

Exercise

Think of the most important nettle you need to grasp.
Grasp it now, or resolve to do so at the first opportunity.

> *Do the right thing and put God first and these other things will also be given to you. (50)*

A THEME A DAY

2

The best way to develop stamina is to do some exercise every day. In spiritual fitness a theme a day keeps the doctor away.

You may have found a daily prayer routine that continues to keep you on your toes, in which case it is best to stick with this. But if you feel a touch of *laissez-faire* coming on, the theme a day approach comes into its own.

There are two ways to choose a theme a day.

You can gather your thoughts, and choose any theme that comes into your mind. For example, you awake shivering on a cold day, frustrated at how little you achieved yesterday, and wishing you could withdraw from the world. You invite inspiration for a theme that speaks to your condition. Into your mind pops these words: 'Give, and you will receive.' So you decide to meditate on the theme of generosity.

You may look up the source of these words and read them in their context. (In this case they are words of Jesus found in the Bible, Luke 6:38.)

Or you can find an anthology. Some of these give a theme, a prayer, suggested Scripture readings and a meditation for each day of the year, perhaps linked to the seasons.

Exercise

Choose a theme, a good quality.

Visualize how this quality was expressed by a person who inspires you or who is featured in the anthology reading.

Pray for this virtue for yourself. Now for others.

Now visualize yourself overflowing in this virtue.

> Every morning you make me eager to hear
> what you wish to teach me. (51)

3
DAILY INPUT ('LECTIO DIVINA')

The Latin phrase 'lectio divina' (the divine reading) has been used for over a thousand years.

It refers to the habit of reading an excerpt from inspired Scripture each day, taking time to reflect on it, and then turning the thoughts this has produced into prayers.

In Christian tradition a psalm, an Old Testament and a New Testament reading are used. The main traditional churches publish a daily lectionary.

A simpler way is to choose one Bible passage each day that speaks to your present situation, or to go through a book in the Bible section by section.

This requires a prayerful, attentive attitude and an openness to God speaking through the Word.

Exercise

1 Choose a passage.

2 Read it slowly several times. Stop at words or phrases that speak to you. Mull them over. Let them sink in. Ask yourself, 'What do I think about this?' and 'What do I feel about this?' Share your thoughts, feelings, questions, hopes with God as you would with a friend.

3 Relax and enjoy God's presence for a while.

4 Write down or remember any key thoughts or feelings the passage has sparked in you, or any action you have been prompted to take. If possible, share these with someone you trust.

All Scripture is inspired by God, and is useful for teaching the truth, pointing out error, correcting faults and instructing in right living (52)

4
A DAILY PRAYER FRAMEWORK

It was Jesus who taught the famous prayer which is now known as the *Our Father* or *The Lord's Prayer*, but it is a prayer that all believers in God can, and do, pray.

It can be said straight through just like this:

Our Father, who is in heaven
May you be honoured
Your kingdom come
Your will be done
On earth as it is in heaven.
Give us this day our daily bread
Forgive us our sins
as we forgive those who sin against us.
Lead us not into temptation
But deliver us from evil
For the kingdom, the power, and the glory are yours
Now and for ever. Amen.

You may find it helpful to learn it by heart.

Scholars believe, however, that Jesus gave these phrases as a framework for prayer. Each phrase can lead us into meditation and intercession over an extended period. It can be used in this way each day of the week through the years.

Here is one such way to use it.

Day 1 – Mondays

'Our Father who is in heaven, may you be honoured.'

Now, and any time throughout the day, think of everyone in your work, home, national situation . . . Picture them honouring God.

Day 2 – Tuesdays

'Your kingdom come, your will be done, on earth as it is in heaven.'

Picture God's will being done on this little bit of earth, right where you are, or where others are for whom you have a concern.

Day 3 – Wednesdays

'Give us our daily bread.'

That is, give us our basic needs for today (don't worry about tomorrow). These may include food, house, job, relationships, purpose.

Day 4 – Thursdays

'Forgive us our sins as we forgive those who sin against us.'

Watch out here. You are meant to start by naming each person you blame for something, or between whom there is a barrier. Forgive them (that does not mean you condone wrongs, or cancel any restitution they ought to make; it means there will no longer be any personal malice towards them). Now you can ask God to forgive you, because you are as bad as the people you have just forgiven – even though not in the same way.

Day 5 – Fridays

'Lead us not into temptation.'

Today there are hundreds of steps you will take. How easy to take wrong steps. So this is a prayer that you will be led to go and say and do right every step of the way.

Day 6 – Saturdays

'But deliver us from evil.'

Maybe you are caught already in a web of some kind – deceit perhaps, or dishonesty or debt or shady practices or pressures – so you pray that God will deliver you from this. The Almighty has been described as 'The God of surprises'; the secret in praying these words is to be ready for a surprise.

Day 7 – Sundays

'For yours is the kingdom, the power and the glory, for ever and ever, Amen.'

These words are a Jewish ending which was added on to prayers of many kinds. It is good to end, not with our problems, but with God's praise. Focus your thoughts on who God is, on the smallness of our affairs, even of this universe, compared to the world of the unseen, the world of eternity, the transforming glory of the divine.

Exercise

Try this for a week.
If it proves helpful, use it for a longer period.

When you pray, don't babble... say 'Our Father...' (53)

5
OVERCOMING HURDLES

If you asked the millions of people who have never climbed anything more than a few stairs to go and climb Mount Everest, it would be a non-starter. But if you asked these same people to climb one more stair each day as preparation for a mass 'fun climb' of a small local mountain, it would be a starter.

Nothing ventured, nothing gained.

If I arrive at my fitness centre on a day when I am weak and cannot lift heavy weights, I do not do nothing, I use the rowing machine. In life there is always a next step we can take.

I like the story of St Patrick's friend Attracta who went to an uninhabited area to start a faith community, and faced one obstacle after another. There were no ropes to pull the timber for the buildings, so she cut off her hair and used that to create a cord! There were no horses to drag the timber, so she made friends with a wild deer and brought it into service. One of the work team drowned, so she dragged him out, prayed over him and nursed him back to fitness.

Exercise

Become aware of the hurdles that lie before you.

Decide on one, realistic hurdle that you will try and overcome today.

> We are more than conquerors through
> God who loved us. (54)

6
STOP THE ROT

When rot or woodworm sets in, it will spread and eventually bring the house down unless action is taken to stop the rot. The action might be to replace the affected items of wood, or to treat them with curative chemicals.

A cancer in our bodies needs to be cut out or reduced through treatment such as radiation.

It is like that with our spiritual condition.

We should not, however, confuse spiritual 'rot' with natural processes such as ageing. That process can be a movement from one plane of energy to a higher plane. 'Rot' refers to something destructive that eats away at eternal qualities in us.

Jesus, speaking symbolically, taught that 'if your eye offends you, pluck it out'. That is, we must root out of our lives anything that obsesses us to the detriment of our own or others lives.

Exercise

Identify what obsessions need to be cut out of your life.

Decide what you will stop doing and thinking.

Confide this to someone you can trust. and ask them to help you stick to your decision.

So help you God.

> *If your hand makes you lose your faith, cut it off! It is better to go through life with one hand than for your whole being to be dumped on the scrap heap. (55)*

7
A.C.T.S.

This spiritual fitness training programme offers great variety. Yet perhaps some trainees are saying to themselves, 'I've had enough of pick and mix; I want a regular, logical routine for my praying, something I can use every day without fuss.'

If that's how you feel, try this.

Exercise

Adore
Confess
Thank
Supplicate

To *adore* God you can use words from hymns, songs, prayers, the Bible. Or you can adore without words.

To *confess* your own sins you can look back over the last day or so and call these to mind. You may confess the human community's sins against the creation, humanity or God that especially upset you. You may mention hurts, sorrows. You may use your own words or a general confession from a prayer book or the words of a song.

To *thank* God properly, don't forget to mention the everyday things without which our lives would be awful, as well as the joys of life, creation and friendship.

To *supplicate* means to keep on asking. It's like knocking on a door until it opens. You can group your requests into those for yourself, for friends, for the world. If you want to be really neat and tidy, you can choose a different area of concern for each day of the week, or month; or, if you are really a tidiness freak, for a year.

Pray in all ways, never give up, and pray
for all God's people. (56)

The
RIGHT WAY
to
PRAY ABOUT . . .

Regular gym users can fool themselves into believing that they are experts simply because they often repeat the same exercises. But a new member who asks a coach to guide them, learns to do each exercise and use each piece of equipment scientifically. Sometimes a small change in the angle of arms or legs makes all the difference. The first person blithely repeats faulty or useless exercises and benefits little. The second person learns the correct ways and overtakes the first in fitness and competence.

It can be like that in life as a whole.

A publisher issued a major book series each of whose titles began 'The right way to . . .' There was a wide range of subjects, but none of them included 'The right way to pray'.

Sometimes we have too vague an idea of prayer. There is no problem or opportunity about which we cannot pray. But each requires know-how. The right angle makes all the difference. This section gives seven examples of issues and how we can intelligently pray about them.

1
TERRORISM

Since September 11, 2001, no part of the world has been immune from the threat of terrorism.

Yet how can we pray about this when both sides regard the other as the real terrorist? It's as dicey as asking God to bless a political party – surely God does not take sides.

The right way to pray about terrorism is to focus on four different needs: The victims, the perpetrators, the causes and ourselves.

First, we place the dead, the injured and bereaved in the presence of the healing compassion of God. After the September 11 tragedy, a schoolgirl's picture of Christ emerging from the crumbling Twin Towers taking souls of the dead into his heart was widely disseminated on the internet. That is a good focus for prayer in such situations.

Second, we place the perpetrators into the same healing presence. But healing means wholeness – they can't hide behind half truths or hatred in eternity. They will have to realize the enormity of what they have done. Pray that they may realize this before they leave this earth, not just afterwards.

Third, we pray into the causes: the anger, hopelessness, injustice or brainwashing that breeds hatred, hardness and violence. Pray that the perpetrators who feel themselves to be victims of western greed and oppression may be understood by those they hit out at. Pray for a non-violent struggle to replace the gods of greed and power within western countries, and that this may bring about a fellowship that spans the two halves of the world.

Fourth, pray for our own responses, that we may handle our emotions such as fear, revenge, resignation, in the way Christ would.

Exercise

Terrorism can paralyse us. Spiritually fit people refuse to be paralysed.

Visualize Christ inviting four people to a round table for his last supper on earth: a wounded victim of a terrorist act, the perpetrator of this act, the leader of the west's anti-terror campaign and yourself.

What does each of them say, do and feel? How does Christ act? Now go and behave like Christ.

Do not let evil defeat you.

Instead, overcome evil with good. (57)

2
FAILED ROMANCE

Your dream has burst. The romance has failed.

The right way to pray is to ask what you can learn: a basis for true love might be just beginning.

In fiction, two people's first feelings of attraction may last forever; in real life they never do. The image of romantic love is a myth.

Sexual impulses are fleeting, and can be aroused with people we are unsuited to. The bloom of romance frequently fades.

Sooner or later each individual will want to use their money, time, friendship and house in ways that conflict with their partner. Then they will realize that they are not, in fact, one.

So the first thing to get clear is this: Do not confuse sexual impulse with true love. If you do, it will always lead to misery.

The second thing to get clear is this: True love lies in doing our best for someone even when we do not feel loving.

When we constantly practice doing this we will find true love and we will grow as human beings. Some people make a romantic contract in order to be dependent upon the other, or to feed their ego. In true love we can live on our own but we choose to share our life with the other. Parasites cannot know true love.

Exercise

Stand with your feet apart, firmly earthed on the ground.

Visualize two paths ahead of you.

The first is the path of misery. This path is to mistake sexual impulses for true love. It leads only to the garbage dump.

The second is the path of true love, the decision to do the best for the other. It is sometimes uphill, but it leads into places of fulfilment.

Now make a choice. Visualize your first steps along the path you have chosen.

If you have chosen the path of true love, stand still and face up to what it may involve:

emotional suffering . . .

the pain involved in facing up to fears . . .

loss of surface ego pleasures . . .

The issue now is this: Have you the will to walk this path?

Make your decision, and walk along your path, visualizing possible experiences.

> To lay your life down for another is
> the greatest form of love. (58)

3
THE CONTROL FREAK

We tend to avoid control freaks. But what about the control freak in ourselves?

'I'll skip this exercise,' you say? Don't be too sure. There's a bit of the control freak in everyone; it's just that when it's in ourselves we call it by nicer names.

So, why not give yourself the benefit of the doubt? On the basis that prevention is better than cure, why not practise the following exercise? It can be fun.

Exercise

Pray along these lines:

Bring to my attention, Lord,
the things I am possessive about . . .
Bring to my attention, Lord,
the ways I arrange things
which rob others of their freedom of choice . . .
Bring to my attention, Lord,
the people I am possessive about . . .

Now start, in your praying mind, to do the opposite of your controlling instinct:

Lord, I give away this (or that) thing . . .
Lord, today help me to fit myself in to someone else's schedule, and to cease trying to fit them in to mine . . .

Lord, I release to you and to others the following people
whom I want for myself
(Name them . . .)
AMEN.

I have learned to be content

whether I have everything

or whether I have nothing (59)

4
LOOMING
TROUBLE

At the time of writing the average person in Britain has 28,453 days to live on earth.

It seems a crime to spoil any one of those days.

What does spoil a day? Many a day is spoilt by worry about past or future troubles.

When serious trouble looms our feelings may cry out in words such as these:

'I feel as if it will overwhelm me.'

'I feel weak, like jelly.'

'I feel crushed, and in pain.'

'I feel threatened, and I want to curl up, surrounded by
spikes like a porcupine, to keep threats away.'

If you face any such situation, remember these words, which echo those of Jesus:

The troubles of today are enough for you.
You do not have to carry tomorrow's troubles.
Let these go.
Bring today's troubles to me.
Pray to me about these and you will find help.

Exercise

Release tomorrow's troubles into the hands of God.

Name each trouble, fear, failure or hurt one by one.

As you name each one visualize it leaving your body and your spirit.

Now pray for today's troubles in words such as these:

Lord, I offer you this day's troubles.
Give me
strength to bear them,
wisdom to handle them,
compassion for those who bring them,
peace as to their outcome.

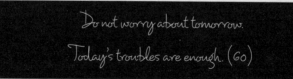

Do not worry about tomorrow.
Today's troubles are enough. (60)

5

SOUR-FACED PEOPLE

Some people are so sour faced that you pass by on the other side in order to keep yourself happy. You avoid eye contact. If a third person observed you, however, they would probably think you were becoming sour faced too. Like begets like.

But prayer changes things. Make this Celtic prayer your own:

Christ be in eye of foe and stranger.

Exercise

Look the first sour-faced person you meet in the eye until your eyes say, 'Christ be in your eyes'.

Smile on them until your smile says, 'Christ be in your heart'.

Suppose they have passed you without a flicker of acknowledgement of your generous prayer? Offer a third prayer on these lines:

Christ be before you.
Christ be ahead of you.
Christ at your homing.
Christ at your dawn.

It can be fun watching out for their first smile.

Try this for several days, and then take it one stage further. Words like these could be a prayer: *Hello, it's nice to see you!*

Kind words bring life:

Cruel words crush the spirit. (61)

6
PARENT-ADULT-CHILD

We come across people who rebel against relatives, work colleagues or leaders. It is not, however, only other people who rebel. Bits of our own lives may be dysfunctional because they have been repressed. It can help to pray for these as if they are rebel members of our own person.

Sometimes a counsellor will advise a client to think of themselves as three jostling personalities:

> the inner child – the undeveloped and emotionally needy me;
>
> the inner parent – the bossy me that says 'ought';
>
> the inner adult – the mature me who behaves appropriately.

Exercise

Perhaps, when you behave unreasonably, you become aware that it is really your inner child crying out for attention, because it has not been heard or affirmed.

The adult in you should then pray for your inner child. Visualize and lay loving hands upon the child within you. Talk to it on these lines: 'I hear you ... I understand you ... I love you ... May goodness fill you ... May peace fill you ... May God enfold you ...'

Perhaps you behave unreasonably because the parent in you has gone into overdrive. Your inner adult can pray for your inner parent. A little humour can help. 'Calm it my dear silly thing, now come and sit down ...'!

But it may be better for your inner child to do the praying. It can put its arms round its parent with words such as 'Come off your hobby horse and let's have a big long hug.' You may see these responses as pale reflections of God's love, and you may feel God's presence in these conversations.

How awful – you are like fancy sepulchres – whitewashed on the outside but inside everything is decayed. (62)

7
RUBBISH

$\mathcal{E}$very sensation, thought and action we have ever experienced – millions of them – is stored in our cells. This means that, as well as much that is good, we accumulate much rubbish. Since all this rubbish is part of ourselves, we can't get rid of it on our own.

But if another human being would volunteer to take away our rubbish so that it becomes his rubbish, and would be able to dispose of it in some way – that would be a breakthrough!

That is why Christians advise that prayers to get rid of our rubbish should be directed to God in Jesus Christ – for he is both truly human and truly divine.

'Rubbish prayers' can be short and simple, but they need to come from the heart.

Exercise

Write a list of those items of inner rubbish you have accumulated which come to mind.

Place this list in a rubbish bin.

Place the rubbish bin in front of a Cross.

Kneel before the Cross and pray:

Foul, I come to be cleaned up.
Naked, I come to be dressed.
Empty, I come to be filled.

Now place the bin the other side of the Cross.

Stand up, turn round, walk away and shout 'I'm free!'

The life blood of God's Son purifies us from every sin. (63)

The
POISE
and the
GRACE

Neither strength, speed nor stamina alone can create poise.

Poise cannot be expressed in words, but we know it when we see it.

Poise and grace grow when the different parts of our physique and character are in good working order and interact appropriately with each other and with the world around.

In order to develop these qualities, we have to eliminate rough edges and angularities and encourage our different parts to work in harmony.

1
USE BEAUTY
SUPPLEMENTS

*I*t is no good getting rid of our rubbish only to fill up our empty lives with new rubbish. Our prayers should regularly include requests to be filled up with good things.

We need to make sure that these prayers are not just words. It would be stupid to drive our cars to filling stations unless we made sure that our tanks were actually filled! It is like that with prayer. Prayer is not just words, but an act of receiving the good Spirit that can be poured into our lives.

The Bible (Galatians 5:22) names nine good things we can receive that are known as 'fruits of God's Spirit'.

Exercises

Breathe deeply, open your hands and your heart, and ask to be filled with one of these fruits:

Fill me with . . .

Love	Joy
Peace	Patience
Kindness	Goodness
Faithfulness	Humility
Restraint	

Take your time in order to let these flow into you as petrol flows in to an empty tank.

What is your favourite flower or scent? Savour it in your mind.

What fragrance in your character do you desire? Winsomeness? Freedom from self concern . . . ? Visualize this fragrance filling you.

> *God says 'I will love my people with all my heart . . . and they shall be alive, beautiful and fragrant.'* (64)

2
GO WITH THE FLOW

*I*t's easy to go with the flow when you are in a Jacuzzi, but how do you do this when you are in a traffic jam or any other sort of jam?

Exercise

Sit back in the car or bus, *and go with the flow of the traffic.*

So it is moving at five miles per hour? That gives you a breathing space. Notice that all the vehicles on your side of the road are going with the flow, in one direction. It is the same the other side of the road.

Bless the traffic. Pray that the drivers and passengers may go with the flow instead of being tense and resistant.

Use this experience as a prod to go deeper.

Go with the flow of the things under the surface of your life.

3
EXPRESS COMPASSION

Think of a person who has given you love that touched you deeply. That person may be a parent, a friend or even a passing stranger.

The love that you felt then can be yours to give to others.

Exercise

Picture love flowing out of you to one person whom you know. Begin with your closest circle. Then extend it.

Now visualize a circle of love around you. Think of a sick or broken person. Draw them into that circle of love. Embrace them. Now turn round and visualize the eternal Being of Love, whom I shall name as Christ. Transfer them from your arms into the arms of this divine Being.

The importance of the transfer is this: Our human love is derived love. Christ's love is uncreated and therefore inexhaustible.

4
SEND OUT GOOD VIBES

Fiona McCleod wrote a long prayer that begins, 'Deep peace of the running wave to you'. Several lines of this prayer were much used on the pilgrim island of Iona and became famous.

But the original prayer is much longer and is based on the idea of transjecting to people the deep peace reflected in different facets of creation.

Just to look at some people makes you feel miserable. That is not surprising, since each person gives out either positive or negative vibes all the time; these can affect whatever or whoever is around.

On a bad day it can seem as if a majority of the population give out bad vibes. This creates a vicious circle, for we tend to reflect back what we receive: an eye for an eye, or a bad vibe for a bad vibe.

Unless we return our vibes through our prayers.

Exercise

Each aspect of creation that contains deep peace finds an echo somewhere within ourselves. Practice locating deep peace somewhere within yourself.

Pray 'peace to you' and transject this to places that are suspicious, ruffled or anxious:

> in yourself
>
> in others
>
> in the world.

Jesus said "Peace be with you.

As my Father sent me,

so I am sending you.' (67)

5

DEVELOP CLING-FREE LIVING

Nothing is more debilitating than being henpecked or being surrounded by grown people who cling to you all the time.

But are we ourselves free from clinging attitudes?

us, we know that this kind of clinging attitude ... ing in us wants to be free, like the sky. The fact ... ometimes our inhibitions steal our aspirations.

... not cling to things, we are free to get up and move ... we do not cling to become free to do the same, for, as far as ... re concerned, we have left them fresh, untouched.

Whenever an emotion arises in us, we can experience either attachment or aversion to it.

The liberated person, however, accepts each emotion without either attachment or aversion, like cars passing by us as we lie in a field contemplating the sky.

Exercise

Visualize yourself lying in a field, contemplating the sky.

Allow to pass before you the persons and things you are tempted to cling to. Let them pass on, and return to enjoying you being you, and the sky being the sky.

To the pure everything is pure. (68)

6
LEARN SERENITY

Things that destroy serenity include
    criticism
    quarrelling

a crumbling framework

unfair demands

'overdrive'

Things that create serenity include

acceptance of what we cannot change

determination to change what we should

wisdom to know the difference

Exercise

Make a list of things that destroy your serenity.

Accept what you cannot change.

Decide to change what you can.

Say this prayer: 'Grant me the serenity of knowing that I do your will.'

> *I am serene.*
>
> *As a child lies quietly in its mother's arms,*
>
> *so my heart is quiet within me. (69)*

7
CONTEMPLATE

A famous priest in the little French village of Ars observed a peasant who every day sat in the church and stared at the crucifix saying nothing. 'What are you doing?' the ...sant replied, 'I just look at him, and he just ...s contemplative prayer.

...ng. Just being. Just feeling the presence of God.

...yer of the heart. It is ceaseless prayer, because it is the he... ...position.

It is the feeling a lover has for her beloved.

The one who contemplates grows in poise and grace. He or she does not notice this. Others do.

Exercise

Sit still.

Visualize your heart being that of a lover.

Visualize the Other, whom you love.

Love without words.

Be.

She sat at Jesus' feet. (70)

Spice
IT UP

Every so often my local gym changes the position of the exercise machines, the colour of the wall paint or the posters. Sometimes it launches a competition or asks us to sponsor a charity event. It encourages us to ring the changes: If we get bored with one routine, try out another. Occasionally some new piece of equipment is introduced.

Variety is the spice of life. This principle applies just as much to our spiritual development.

In this section we suggest ways to vary and add spice to our spiritual routines, such as laughter.

1
LAUGHTER

In 1999 a survey* revealed that Italians laugh an average of nineteen minutes a day, the British laugh fifteen minutes, but the Germans only laugh for six minutes. This news was so serious that a German citizen established Laughter Clubs.

The first exercise folk do at these clubs is to laugh with their mouth. The second exercise is to laugh with their hearts.

To laugh with your heart is to pray. This is not as easy as you think. You need to lubricate the heart and warm it up.

Exercise

Let's start on the outside and move to the inside.

Count 3 . . . Start laughing *now!* Keep practising this until it becomes second nature.

The same technique can work with the heart. Imagine it is like a light switch that you suddenly turn on.

Count 3 . . . Start laughing with the heart *now!*

Now think of five coming occasions that make you gloomy. Imagine them now, and do the laugh with the heart exercise.

Repeat this when you actually get to the miserable occasion.

Laughter prayer does good like a medicine.

God's kingdom is like a party (71)

*Research carried out in Berkeley, California, recorded in *The Week*, 20 February 1999.

2
STONES

The great sculptor Michelangelo looked long at a piece of raw marble to see what was 'in' it; he then visualized the shape that he could chisel out of it. Saint Paul wrote that we are like living stones, each one has our own individuality, our own potential for building a better world.

Choose a stone and look long and hard at it. What jumps out at you as you contemplate it? What quality that you desire does it speak of? You can turn this into a prayer: 'Make me a living stone of _____ (name a quality).'

Exercise

Gather five stones and place them in a circle.

Take the first stone in your hand. This is the stone of earth. We are meant to be people of the earth. Hildegaard of Bingen says, 'Holy people draw the earth to themselves.'

Silently hold the stone, breathe in the air deeply and meditate on these words:

May we enter into our earthiness.

Place the first stone on the ground.

Take the second stone in your hand.

This is the stone of peace. We are meant to be people of peace. Jesus says, 'Blest are the peacemakers'. Silently hold the stone, breathe in the air deeply and meditate on these words:

Deep peace of the quiet earth.
Deep peace of the still air.

Deep peace of the setting sun.
Deep peace of the Son of peace.

Place the second stone on the ground.

Take the third stone in your hand.

This is the stone of hospitality. We are meant to be givers of hospitality. The Scriptures teach that by giving hospitality, we entertain angels without knowing it. Silently hold the stone, breathe in the air deeply and meditate on these words:

I would prepare a feast and be host to the great High King,
with all the company of heaven.
The sustenance of pure love be in my house,
the roots of repentance in my house.
Baskets of love be mine to give,
with cups of mercy for all the company.
Sweet Jesus, be there with us, with all the company of
heaven.
May cheerfulness abound in the feast,
the feast of the great High King,
my host for all eternity.

Traditional Irish prayer

Place the third stone on the ground.

Take the fourth stone in your hand.

This is the stone of healing. We are meant to be healing people. Saint James says, 'Pray for one another that you may be healed.' Silently hold the stone, breathe in the air deeply and meditate on these words:

May these be the healing hands of God.

Place the fourth stone on the ground.

Take the fifth stone in your hand.

This is the stone of blessing. We are meant to bless the world. Jesus says, 'It is more blest to give than to receive.'

Silently hold the stone, breathe in the air deeply and meditate on these words:

Bless the earth that is beneath me
Bless the sky that is above me
Bless the folk who live around me
Bless your image deep within me.

Place the fifth stone on the ground, so that the five stones now make a circle.

Walk sunwise around the circle several times, singing, humming or praying silently.

> Jesus said, 'Even the stones will start to shout.' (72)

3
RAP

*I*n rap music a person makes up words as he or she goes along, and somehow the rhythm of the beat draws out the words and keeps the flow going.

Freestyle rap is individual and fresh, the words come from the inside of a person. It is not great art; it will not be written down and copied by others.

There is a way to pray that is like rap. You walk around and say what comes into your mind, aiming to keep to some kind of beat or rhyme. It's fun, it's not heavy, it keeps moving, but it's also real and comes from the heart.

Some may feel too embarrassed to try this, or fear that no words will come. But why not have a go? Remember, it does not matter if you get stuck; just pause and start again. The important thing is that the words come out of your heart.

To show the sort of thing I mean, I will make a fool of myself and record (without artificial 'improvements') some rap words I spoke on January 6. That day is known as Epiphany, the day three wise men found Christ, and the Light of God began to spread all over the world:

> *On this day of Epiphany*
> *I open my arms and I bend my knee*
> *I say 'You're welcome' to the Light flooding in*
> *And I tell my soul 'Where have you been*
> *Hiding yourself in the dark and the cold*
> *Come right out and be right bold!*
> *The Light has come for good, don't you know?*
> *So stop your murm'ring, come on, lets go!'*

Exercise

Go to a place where you feel comfortable and start to rap out loud.

If you are shy, do it in a car or room with a radio that blankets your own voice.

Now start to rap!

Tell everyone the Lord is great
And me they'll always appreciate. (73)

TRAVEL

If Julie, a staff member of my fitness centre, sees me sitting still on a bike machine she shouts, 'Go on'.

It is good to go on, to travel.

Most of us spend a significant proportion of our time travelling – by cycle or car, bus or train, foot, ferry or plane.

We can use the experience of travel to help us pray in several ways.

First, we can use our experience of travel as a picture of life. It is creative to picture our life as a journey.

Columbanus once said, 'I am always moving from the day of birth to the day of death … We must travel as guests of the world.'

Second, we can change the circuits of our mind and body as we experience different patterns of life.

Exercise

Make an inner pilgrimage to a holy or creative place. Visualize what you leave behind, great souls you talk to, fresh perspectives you get.

> Hearing good news from a distant land is like a cool drink when you are thirsty. (74)

5
SIGHTS AND
SOUNDS

God imagined the world before bringing it into existence. Since we are made in God's image, we too are meant to imagine things and to be co-creators with God.

Words alone are not enough. If they were, Jesus, the eternal Word and Image of God, would not have become incarnate in a human being at whom people could look.

Icons on our computers reveal something without having to use words, but what they reveal is only a pointer to what is there when we open it up.

It is like that with icons of the Christian church.

Since the Invisible God (whom people were told not to make images of) chose to become visible, many Christians have found it helpful to look at a representation of Christ, of angels or of saintly Christians who inspire us.

Tradition says that Saint Luke painted pictures of Jesus' mother on cave walls. One is still preserved in Malta. The early Christians carved pictures in Rome's underground catacombs where, during times of persecution, they secretly met to pray. Since the great icon of Christ was placed in Saint Catherine's monastery in Sinai 1300 years ago, the making of icons has flourished, at first in the east, and now also in the west.

Exercise

Open an illustrated Bible or look at an icon of Christ or of a messenger of Christ.

Gaze at it long enough to sense the awe and mystery of the unseen Presence of God. Then invite the Holy Spirit to open a window into this unseen Presence.

> *Fill your minds with whatever things are true, pure and beautiful. (75)*

6
OIL

When some seafaring monks feared they would hit troubled waters and be shipwrecked, their leader, Aidan of Lindisfarne, gave them a jar of blessed oil. 'If the waves threaten to overwhelm you, pour this oil on them and they will subside,' he told them with prophetic insight.

This is exactly what happened. As they poured the oil over the pounding waves, the wind and the storm subsided.

This story is the origin of the time honoured English phrase 'to pour oil on troubled waters'.

The world is in a sea of troubles. We can learn in our prayers to pour oil on troubled waters.

Call to mind 'troubled waters' in your life or in the world.
Visualize yourself pouring oil on these.

Also visualize yourself pouring oil to sweeten hostile people,
freshen stale situations or heal festering wounds.

> *You do not realise how miserable and*
> *pitiful you are ... buy some oil. (76)*

7
HEALTH FARMS

Nowadays many people take a break at a health farm, a meditation
centre – or a monastery, which is a form of a spiritual health farm.

But suppose you find yourself in a monastery that uses chants.
How do you pray with monks like that? Their kind of prayer seems
the opposite of the 'choose from the menu' or 'follow the thoughts
of your heart' type of prayer.

To join in with them you have to say a lot of words, and not
when you want to, but at set times. You have to fit your own
thoughts into their pattern whether or not you feel like it.

Still, if you're there for the ride, you might as well make the best
of it. After all, athletes get into training routines, and successful
business people accept the disciplines of their profession.

Exercise

If you're able, pray with monks. When they read Scriptures, focus all your attention on what the Scripture says. When they offer praise, remember that they are giving devotion to God as a Person they love very much. Imagine you are doing the same. When they pray for others, put yourselves in the shoes of the people they pray for.

When you get 'information overload', stop trying to concentrate and let the words flow over you like the spray from a waterfall until you are ready to concentrate again.

There will be pauses for silence. Use these pauses to sort out your thoughts and think about the words that had most impact on you.

Get into the habit of praying with these monks. As you do so, visualize people praying like them across the world, across the ages and across heaven. You are tuning in to a channel that is always broadcasting. This might prove to be the channel for you.

Day by day the early Christians met together in the temple and said the Prayers. (77)

Strong STUFF

Body builders and power lifters come in all sizes, but one thing is for sure: they have to strain every muscle, make this their priority and go to their limits. It's not for every one. It's strong stuff.

There are some parallels in spiritual fitness. This section is strong stuff. If you do not want to wield a sword, or if it makes you queasy, skip it. Or come back to this part later when you're ready for the strong stuff.

1
HELL HOLES

The hells of this world are many. By instinct we try to avoid them. Yet, as we grow in compassion, a desire to pray for people in these hell holes may grow in us. How can we pray?

According to the New Testament, Jesus Christ descended into the place of tormented spirits and tried to bring them back with him into a place of freedom, peace and light (1 Peter 3:19).

This provides us with an image that we can use in our prayer.

Exercise

In your imagination go to a hell hole, such as a war-torn or disaster area.

Pray that divine help may come to those trapped there.

Pray for the children, that guardian angels may surround them.

Pray for any who have caused this hell (armed enemies, perhaps) that they may move away from hatred towards humanity.

Pray that goodness may over come evil, love may overcome hatred and life may overcome death.

> The kingdoms of this world have become
> the kingdom of our God. (78)

ANGEL POWER

²

*I*n the *Star Wars* films the phrase 'May the Force be with you' indicates that the heroes can be in touch with a force infinitely more intelligent and pervasive than their own. However, what prevents them from harnessing that force is pride, jealousy and the desire to build their own empire.

Great champions for Christ have harnessed God's angels to the task of building his empire. Patrick of Ireland (fifth century) was one of these. The prayer attributed to him, known as St Patrick's Breastplate, which has already been quoted, calls on God's angels. It contains these words:

> *I arise today*
> *through the vast strength of heaven*
> *through the strength of the love of cherubim*
> *in the obedience of angels*
> *in the service of archangels*
> *in the hope of resurrection to meet with reward.*

Exercise

Visualize the cosmos with God, the Supreme Being, at its height and centre. Emanating each side from this centre like a phalanx are indomitable, uncorrupted beings of light, intelligence and energy. There are different levels or orders who carry out different functions.

Now become aware of a challenge ahead of you or the world which seems beyond human solution.

Call upon the field of angels. Visualize yourself arising with the phalanx accompanying you, beside, before and behind.

March into the centre of this evil situation. Visualize what happens. Now do it for real in the first tough situation you walk into.

> *Lord my God, you will come bringing all your angels with you.* (79)

3
THE WARRIOR

In many parts of the Western world young men feel emasculated. Some explore New Age or Old Age rituals which glorify the warrior.

There is another spiritual tradition that neither neuters nor glorifies the warrior spirit; it transforms it onto a higher plane.

The Celtic Christian tradition, for example, identifies Christ as a spirit warrior who fights against evil in and outside human beings.

The legends of the chivalrous 'King' Arthur who defeats with his sword Excalibur those who mistreat good people is an abiding image for many.

To become a spiritual warrior is to develop qualities of courage, intelligence and initiative.

Exercise

Visualize yourself swishing an Excalibur-like sword.

Cut off the relationships and activities in your life that are not right.

Cut through red tape, lies, phoney and underhand ways, with the sword of truth.

Now identify something wrong that you will encounter today or tomorrow: 'Put on' God's armour now, and go prepared to do something positive.

> Put on God's armour.
>
> Wear truth as your belt and wield the sword of the Spirit of God's living word so that you will be able to repel all the enemy's missiles. (80)

4

THE TONGUE TAMER

How many of the trillions of words that humans have uttered since the dawn of history have been thoughtless, unclean or unkind?

How many of our own words have been thus?

Human beings have been able to tame wild animals and birds, reptiles and fish, but no human being can tame the tongue.

James the Elder

Do you wish you could tame the tongue?

When you speak, would you like each word to count and to bring something positive to the hearers?

Exercise

Visualize a time before the creation of this universe when there was a silent void, nothing.

Then a 'Word' comes forth from this void. Each time the Word speaks, it expresses what it means and brings this into being.

Light emerges. Matter emerges. Vegetation emerges. Creatures emerge. Humans emerge.

The Word is energy, life, differentiation.

Now envisage the transitory nature of all that is created. When you are ready, envisage, in contrast, the eternal power of a word you speak in love or truth.

Remain in silent contemplation of the power of the Word.

When you are ready, make a vow to keep silent throughout this day, except when something needs to be said. And to say what needs to be said with thought and love, being fully present to the person you are speaking to.

Look out for an increase in the quality of the day.

> Make sure your conversation is always pleasant and with a touch of humour, and is appropriate to what each person needs. (81)

5
FORGIVENESS FROM THE HEART

Whom do I need to forgive?

Any person or group of persons who has, through words, looks, deeds or neglect, done any of the following to myself or those I care about:

excluded   belittled

blocked   stolen a partner

robbed   abused

failed to honour an agreement

ignored our needs

Exercise

Say the following aloud:

I acknowledge that I am hurt (or angry).
Slowly rehearse the things which have hurt you.
In your mind now (and later say audibly whatever is appropriate), say the following to the person or group who has caused the hurt:

I acknowledge that you are both a hurter and a person (or group) in need.
I ask God to deal with you as is best for you.
I will communicate to you the effect your treatment has had on me (or us) if this will help.
Now I forgive you with my lips.

*In my mind I look you in the eyes, and I say 'I forgive you'
with my eyes.*

Ask the Holy Spirit (that is, the Spirit who makes whole) to turn
your words also into feelings. Take time, if possible, to let this
change take place in you. If there is not enough time, trust that this
change will take place in due course.

Now say the following:

*I look into my heart, and I forgive you with my heart.
Go in peace.*

If ever the old unforgiving attitude comes back, repeat the exercise.

> *Whoever has been forgiven only a little
> shows only a little love. (82)*

6
EMERGENCY CALL

I left at 4.30 a.m. for what I thought was 'an important engage-
ment'. Knowing that there were extensive works on the main road, I
detoured and arrived back on the A road near the final section of
road works. Unfortunately, I discovered I could only travel along it
one way – the wrong way. So, since the road was quiet at such an
early hour, I hit on the bright idea of driving between two cones in
the middle of the carriageway and driving a little up the other side
until the road works finished.

Unfortunately for my car I had not noticed a deep trench between the two halves of the carriageway. I drove into this and was unable to move the car. The rear end stuck out within inches of a huge container vehicle veering down on me along the single file bit of road.

How does one pray in such an emergency? Here are the sequences I went through.

'Help me to act as Jesus would,' I prayed as I leapt out of the car and ensured the oncoming driver did not hit my car.

I was aware of panic, which leads to confusion. 'Keep me calm,' I asked, and peace set in. I put cones around my car and, after several attempts to reverse the car, decided that course of action was futile.

I was about to run in all directions, but God said 'stand back'. I looked for signs of another road or house. There were no signs. 'Don't try and be independent. Accept that you are vulnerable and that you need help,' God told me.

I used St Patrick's Breastplate, which invites the help of the hosts of heaven. 'Send an angel please,' I asked him. The angels came quickly, in the form of two smiling, uniformed police officers.

They phoned for two other colleagues, and supervised the oncoming traffic until their colleagues arrived.

There was quite a long wait. Would it be a garage job? Would the car start?

I tried the circling prayer, circling the car, the road, the police, and the breakdown people who were hopefully on their way.

I was about to give thanks for the help of the police but God asked, 'What lessons do you need to learn?' First, I promised God that on a long journey in future I would take a mobile phone, even though I detest them. Second, I admitted I was impetuous, and that I would pray before, not after, acting impetuously in future, so help me God. Third, I said sorry for creating unnecessary wear and tear.

Their colleagues phoned for a breakdown rescue and waited until they had done their job.

I drove off, and then I realized the most important prayer of all must now begin – saying thank you!

Exercise

Recall or visualize an emergency.

Go through the prayers and actions which, in the light of the above experience, you would make.

> *God is a very present help in trouble.* (83)

7
LAST DAY

The Christian faith teaches us to live this day as if it is our last.

This is not morbid. It puts things in perspective. It can be liberating.

It is best to start doing this when we are young.

Exercise

Imagine you are to leave this earth today.*

What things are most important?

What things pale into insignificance?

*This exercise is similar to one of many such as in the author's book *Before We Say Goodbye: Preparing for a Good Death* (HarperCollins).

Who do you need to share something with?

What do you need to say sorry for?

What will you most regret not having achieved?

At the end of your meditation ask yourself: 'In the light of eternal perspectives, what must I cut out, do, put right, communicate today?'

Our days are as grass—(84)

This is not
THE END

This training course is a beginning. You now have enough experience to venture out into deeper waters, such as an awareness of our mortality. Our bodies grow old and perish. The solar system itself is running down.

You may ask, 'When I am oppressed by the thought that nothing lasts, how do I respond?'

Do not run away from this awareness. Embrace it.

Slowly go through the following list. Repeat, 'It will not last', after each item.

> The neurons of the brain
>
> My partner
>
> My house
>
> My job
>
> My body
>
> The earth beneath me
>
> The air I breathe

'How, then, can I find happiness?' you ask.

Two spiritual traditions give different answers to this question.

> Answer one: Things are a mirage. They have no essence. Therefore do not take them seriously.
>
> Answer two: Things are a passing reflection of an eternal reality. Use them as pointers.

You can find happiness when that which is perishable has 'put on' that which is imperishable.

Practice moving from the transient to the eternally real.
Throughout this day, repeat these words:

Lead me from what fades to Eternal Life.
Lead me from what is false to Eternal Truth .
Lead me from what destroys to Eternal Goodness.
Lead me from what divides to Eternal Love.

$\mathcal{I}$f something has happened to you while working with this book, please do not keep it to yourself. Give this or a new copy of the book to someone else.

Sources of Quotations

The quotation at the end of each training session is the author's paraphrase of a text from one of the sixty-six books of the Bible.

The references relate to the title of the book, the chapter and the verse(s).

(1) Isaiah 30:15
(2) Malachi 4:2
(3) Matthew 6:34
(4) Mark 12:31
(5) Luke 16:10
(6) Psalm 51:12
(7) John 5:35
(8) Lamentations of Jeremiah 3:23
(9) Song of Songs 2:10
(10) 1 Peter 5:5
(11) Matthew 24:31
(12) Isaiah 40:31
(13) Ephesians 3:18
(14) Matthew 6:19–21
(15) Luke 11:4
(16) Isaiah 35:6
(17) Psalm 125:2
(18) 1 Thessalonians 5:18
(19) Matthew 6:26, 28
(20) Psalm 150:6
(21) Song of Songs 8:14
(22) Mark 12:30, 31
(23) Ephesians 6:6
(24) 2 Chronicles 6:14
(25) Psalm 121:1
(26) Leviticus 26:6
(27) John 1:47–48
(28) Echoes Psalm 84

(29) Acts 20:35
(30) John 10:10
(31) Isaiah 53:4–5
(32) Psalm 131:2
(33) Philippians 2:4
(34) Hebrews 10:25
(35) Isaiah 26:8
(36) Jeremiah 31:26
(37) Luke 4:18
(38) Matthew 7:1
(39) Matthew 5:10
(40) Psalm 42:3–5
(41) Luke 23:43
(42) Deuteronomy 33:27
(43) Psalm 44:3
(44) 1 Peter 3:4
(45) Philippians 1:9
(46) Malachi 4:2
(47) John 15:14, 16
(48) 1 John 3:1
(49) Proverbs 17:22
(50) Matthew 6:33
(51) Isaiah 50:4
(52) 2 Timothy 3:16–17
(53) Matthew 6:7, 9
(54) Romans 8:37
(55) Mark 9:43
(56) Ephesians 6:18

(57) Romans 12:21
(58) John 15:13
(59) Philippians 4:11–12
(60) Matthew 6:34
(61) Proverbs 15:4
(62) Matthew 23:27
(63) 1 John 1:7
(64) Hosea 14:4, 6
(65) Psalm 78:14
(66) 1 Corinthians 13:7
(67) John 20:21
(68) Titus 1:15
(69) Psalm 131:2
(70) Luke 10:39
(71) Matthew 22:2
(72) Luke 19:40
(73) Luke 1:47–48
(74) Proverbs 25:25
(75) Philippians 4:8
(76) Revelation 3:17–18
(77) Acts 2:42
(78) Revelation 11:15
(79) Zechariah 14:5
(80) Ephesians 6:14–16
(81) Colossians 4:6
(82) Luke 7:47
(83) Psalm 46:1
(84) Psalm 103:15

We want to hear from you. Please send your comments about this book to us in care of zreview@zondervan.com. Thank you.

GRAND RAPIDS, MICHIGAN 49530 USA

WWW.ZONDERVAN.COM